Letters
from the Front
1914–1918

By the same author

War and Military History
Middle East Journey
Return to Glory
One Man's War
Digger (Story of the Australian Soldier)
Scotland the Brave (Story of the Scottish Soldier)
Jackboot (Story of the German Soldier)
Face of War
British Campaign Medals
Codes and Ciphers
The Walking Wounded
Swifter Than Eagles (Biography of Marshal of the R.A.F.
Sir John Salmond)
Anzacs at War
Boys in Battle
Links of Leadership
Tommy Atkins (Story of the English Soldier)
Women in Battle
Jack Tar (Story of the English Seaman)
Surgeons in the Field
Americans in Battle

General
The Hunger to Come (The Food and Population Crises)
Crime and Adventure
Jungle Manhunt
The Devil's Emissary
The Dance of San José
Murder on Flight 354
Murder by Bamboo
I'll Die Tonight
Death has my Number
Crime on my Hands
My Brother's Executioner
Doorways to Danger
New Geography 1966–7
New Geography 1968–9
New Geography 1970–1
Anatomy of Captivity (Political prisoners)

Letters
from the Front
1914–1918

Selected and edited by

John Laffin

J. M. Dent & Sons Ltd London

First published 1973
© John Laffin, 1973

Made in Great Britain at the
Aldine Press · Letchworth · Hertfordshire
for J. M. Dent & Sons Ltd
Aldine House · Bedford Street · London

ISBN 0 460 07854 2

Contents

1 The Hearts of Men at War   1

2 'A Grand Opportunity'   12

3 'Nature makes flags out of anything'   21

4 'Oh Lord, the mystery of men's feelings'   30

5 'An extraordinary elation'   38

6 'A hamper from Harrods weekly' (1915):
'I shall never look on warfare as fine or sporting again.'
(1917) 51

7 'The attack was glorious'   58

8 'Men at war become more bestial'   68

9 'It seemed like a dream'   80

10 'Aren't you sick of it, Fritz?'   90

11 'We need women who are shameless in their pity'   102

12 'America can't imagine the terrible realities'   110

Epilogue: 'The nightmare is gone'   127

Acknowledgments   128

Index   131

I
The Hearts of Men at War

War, as military historians know, is a difficult thing to describe. If the writer goes too deeply into its human anguish he runs the risk of being considered sensational. If he appears to concentrate too much on the heroism of soldiers he will almost certainly be accused of glorifying war. And if his focus is on leadership, tactics and strategy he inevitably gives the impression of being concerned with men as mere numbers and not as human beings.

The many Great Captains who have published their memoirs rarely succeed in describing war. Their books are full of revelations of intrigue, rivalries, strategical considerations, justifications and rationalizations. War for a general is largely intellectual—as it must be. Even the letters of a general to his wife tend to be vague about the realities of war because war to him is mostly taking place on his maps and in his preoccupation with logistics. He is *at* the war but not *of* it.

This was certainly the case in the Great War 1914–18, when even the general commanding a division—on paper, about 20,000 men—was rarely in the firing-line. Generals ran risks, they became casualties, but they did not live under the same conditions as their men and there was no good reason why they should. Still, they should have known of their troops' privations; many generals on their first forays to the front were appalled at what the men were suffering.

This remoteness and preoccupation perhaps explains why so few generals refer to the human—or inhuman—aspect of the Great War, beyond the stock phrases of 'great hardships endured with fortitude' or 'our troops found the winter of 1914–15 rather severe'.

Again, almost any Great War book written in retrospect, even by men who endured four years of front-line hell, suffers from the built-in handicap of retrospection. Depending on the personality of the writer there is a tendency to pitch the horror in low key, perhaps because the author's mental protective mechanism is obscuring some of the worst of his experiences, or to amplify the horror to the point where the reader's distaste prevents his imagination from fully grasping the word picture being painted for him.

All books are those of *survivors*. And in surviving a catastrophe a man's attitude to it becomes subtly changed. The sheer misery becomes something he would 'not have missed for worlds'—though at the time he probably fervently wished himself anywhere else.

Photographs of war are often starkly honest but even they cannot reveal soldiers' emotions and thoughts, their pain and their total exhaustion. Pictures can show death—but not the apprehension of death.

Oral retrospective accounts of war are only peripherally valuable. As a military historian I have spoken at length with men who fought in many of the operations of the Great War. Generally their information is grossly unreliable, though not from deliberate deception. Their own focus was extremely narrow, they were victims of the propaganda of their own side, they tend to make unwarrantable assumptions from sketchy evidence, they exaggerate their own importance in actions and, quite simply, their memories are faulty. In addition, cold, hunger, fear and pain all combined to distort impressions at the time.

The historian must make much use of official records, photographs, memoirs and orally transmitted information in assembling the bones of history. But contemporary letters are his best source of 'field' information. Letters have the enormous value of not having been written for publication; they are therefore spontaneous, sincere and unaffected. It must have been a rare soldier who thought while penning a letter home that it might one day appear in a book or be used as historical evidence. The man writing from the trenches to parents, wife or friend was living only for the day and hoping to survive until his next home leave. Also, because he was writing to intimates he could be frank; there is nothing to suggest that field censorship in any way inhibited letter-writing in the Great War.

Of course, much of the material in letters is subjective—and subjective evidence is sometimes suspect. I consider that it has great validity in relation to war. The value of objectivity in writings on war should be confined to political cause and effect and to the inter-involvement of nations. War at battalion or front-line level can never be objective; it is necessarily a heightened subjective experience involving all the recognized senses and other indefinable ones that only a combat soldier knows about.

The letters which form this collection have been selected from many thousands on the basis of historical interest, intellectual viewpoint, value of description, revelation of feeling and personality, and attitude to the war. I have chosen them as a collection to give a picture of their time and to reveal men and minds rather different from those of more than half a century later.

The majority of the letters are from junior officers, the most articulate men of the armies of 1914–18. The rank and file of the Great War, especially in the British and French armies, were ill-educated and often only functionally literate. Their letters reflect in equal parts their concern for their families and their own paucity of expression. They *felt*—as their officers were sometimes astonished to find out—but they could not express themselves.*

We have direct evidence from the platoon and company officers, whose duty it was to censor their men's mail, of the mundane nature of most letters. Second-Lieutenant A. D.

* See also Stephen Hewett's letters, Chapter 7.

Gillespie, serving in the Argyll and Sutherland Highlanders,[1] wrote to his parents on 3 March 1915, from a trench in France :*

> I have been censoring the men's letters—it seems almost too bad to read them all, but . . . one is glad to know what they are really like, under a rather unpromising surface. One wrote to his wife, thanking her for a shirt, but saying he wished she was here to 'scratch his back as she used to do'! Most of them just want 'so and so' to know they were 'asking' for them.

And again on 7 March, 1915:

> I notice when I am censoring letters that men don't write to their fathers very often, but to mothers and sisters a great deal, and also to 'dear old pals'. It's a shame somehow to read all their letters, but they do write and write, even if it's only to say 'hoping this finds you well, as it leaves me'.

A week later he commented :

> . . . The men's letters [are] often very amusing, but they write so many that it takes up quite a lot of time—they send so many kisses, often to three different girls by the same post, and they are fond of quoting poetry copied from cigarette cards, or some- times their own composition—and there are the usual Scotch phrases, 'lang may your lum reek'.

The correspondence of, say, German and Australian rank and file was quite different—the one often revealing fine sensitivity, the other a breezy, vigorous confidence. As a generalization, the letters of Americans were permeated with an engagingly direct approach to war and life, with sentiment and bloodthirstiness.

One thing is very clear : the letters from the educated men of the Great War were infinitely better written than those of their counterparts of World War II. For one thing, they are com- petently constructed—as if the writers had been inspired with a love of letter-writing at school. Their letters are interesting, fluent and ordered.

* See end of chapter for further biographical notes.

Also, these earlier letters show a quite unselfconscious erudition, with quotations in Latin or Greek, as well as the more expected references from Shakespeare and Milton.

The soldier writers of 1914–18 were thinkers. On 1 December, 1916, Keith Henderson, a young artist turned infantry officer,[2] wrote to his wife:

> [This is] a beautiful cathedral town.
> With doors all padded up with sand-bags, the great cathedral towers above the town, and is seen for miles and miles. A good effort. What fun they must have had building it. What they believed then they expressed in outward and visible form. What we think now is (or ought to be) very different indeed from what they thought then. But I can't remember having ever seen anything that begins to express what we think (or ought to think) now.
>
> Everyone in the Church of England now seems to me to think *almost exactly* what was thought when this cathedral was built! If this war achieves nothing else, I pray with all my mind, and all my soul, and all my strength, that all the sects and all the churches may suddenly feel tired of all the 1001 little methods of procedure, and say: 'Damn it all! what does all this ancient paraphernalia mean to us? Is God quite so complicated and involved as we have supposed? Everything else in the world progresses. Thought progresses. Let us take a deep breath, and realize that religion ought to be more "into the future" than even Zeppelins or Tanks, please.'

Henderson's critical reflectiveness was not unusual. Soldiers of his war pondered, in their letters, on profundities of theology, complexities of politics, convolutions of psychology and a hundred other topics almost completely absent from the letters of soldiers one generation later.

Perhaps most importantly the letters of the Great War are sensitive and responsive. The writers express their fear and despair and equally their sense of joy and happiness; they held back very little of themselves and clearly felt no embarrassment in confessing to emotions which the next generation of fighting men would not have disclosed for fear of being considered soppy.

Lance-Corporal Harold Chapin of the Royal Army Medical Corps,[3] wrote to his wife on 4 May, 1915:

> . . . Eh, bien, I can't express it. I feel as if for a week past a great super-human artist had been painting for me, in all the colours and sounds and feelings and scents of creation, a picture of himself. He is Reality one moment, Mystery the next.

A German student, Eduard Bruhn,[4] mortally wounded on 17 September, 1915, in Russia, found the strength to scrawl a last note to his parents:

> I am lying on the battle-field badly wounded. Whether I recover is in God's hands. If I die, do not weep. I am going blissfully home. A hearty greeting to you all once more. May God soon send you peace and grant me a blessed home-coming. Jesus is with me, so it is easy to die. In heartfelt love,
>
> Eduard.

On 1 July, 1916, before going into the Somme holocaust, Second-Lieutenant John Engall of the 16th London Regiment,[5] wrote to his parents:

> I'm writing this letter the day before the most important moment of my life . . . I took my Communion yesterday with dozens of others who are going over tomorrow; and never have I attended a more impressive service. I placed my body in God's keeping, and I am going into battle with His name on my lips, full of confidence and trusting implicitly in Him. I have a strong feeling that I shall come through safely; but, nevertheless, should it be God's holy will to call me away I am quite prepared to go . . . I could not pray for a finer death; and you, my dear Mother and Dad, will know that I died doing my duty to my God, my Country and my King. I ask that you should look upon it as an honour that you have given your son for the sake of King and Country.

In the face of such faith it is lamentable to record that Lieutenant Engall was killed within the next three days.

All but a few of the men whose letters appear in this book were killed in action. This should make what they have to say all the more important—most of them had nothing else to leave us. And what they have left us is nothing less than the truth. Letters written on the spot have an honesty that is both coldly clear and heatedly impassioned. The truth may be simply a frank admission of an outlook on war. Captain the Hon. Julian Grenfell [6] expressed such an attitude when he wrote to his mother on 24 October, 1914:

> . . . I *adore* war. It is like a big picnic without the objectlessness of a picnic. I have never been so well or so happy.

Another young British officer, Lieutenant Kenneth Garnett,[7] shared Grenfell's opinion when he wrote to his mother in November 1915. With a whole year's war behind him he could say:

> This is all a great game—so very childish—but I am such a child as to love it. . . . Do you remember the fort at Sea View near the Point that the Curwens and I once built? This game is just like that, only more people are playing at it and we don't get into a row for getting our clothes messy. We have our peep-holes just the same, and fire at anything we like—only this, as I said, is much more fun—but it is the same game!

The great game killed him less than two years later.

In contrast to these young Englishmen's adoration of war was the detestation of a young French soldier, a painter turned infantryman, writing to his mother on 21 September, 1914.[8]

> War is rain.
>
> It is suffering beyond what can be imagined. Three days and three nights without being able to do anything but tremble and moan, and yet, in spite of all, perfect service must be rendered.
>
> To sleep in a ditch full of water has no equivalent in Dante, but what can be said of the awakening, when one must watch for the moment to kill or to be killed!
>
> Above, the roar of the shells drowns the whistling of the wind. Every instant, firing. Then one crouches in the mud, and despair takes possession of one's soul.
>
> When this torment came to an end I had such a nervous collapse that I wept without knowing why—late, useless tears.

The truth about war may be a reasoned but vehement plea for sanity, as it was from Captain Theodore Cameron Wilson,[9] writing to a friend, Mrs Orpen, on 3 May, 1916.

[War] makes one see this Spring's evening beauty through a sort of veil of obscenity, as a madman may see beauty. For mangled bodies are obscene, whatever war-journalists may say. *War* is an obscenity. Thank God we are fighting to stop war. Otherwise very few of us could go on. Do teach your dear kids the horror of responsibility which rests on the war-monger. I want so much to get at children about it. We've been wrong in the past. We have *taught* schoolboys 'war' as a romantic subject. We've made them learn the story of Waterloo as a sort of exciting story in fiction. And everybody has grown up soaked in the poetry of war—which exists, because there is poetry in everything, but which is only a tiny part of the great dirty tragedy. All those picturesque phrases of war writers—such as 'he flung the remnants of his Guard against the enemy', 'a magnificent charge won the day' are dangerous because they show nothing of the *individual* horror, nothing of the fine personalities smashed suddenly into red beastliness, nothing of the sick fear that is tearing at the hearts of brave boys who ought to be laughing at home—a thing infinitely more terrible than physical agony. . . . It isn't death we fear so much as the long-drawn expectation of it—the sight of other fine fellows ripped horribly out of existence by 'reeking shard' as a great War-journalist says who spoke (God forgive him) of 'a fine killing' in some battle or other.

The killing was so wholesale that between 1914 and 1918 no fewer than 15,000,000 servicemen were killed in battle or died of their wounds. These few letters cannot be entirely representative of so many men of so many nationalities. But they do halt the flow of history, freezing it so that we can see the fighting men of the Great War under the bright light they themselves focus by their letters.

To preserve a narrative editorial thread I have, as far as possible, ordered these letters chronologically but in the case of soldiers represented by more than one letter I have kept them together. However, one letter speaks so impartially for soldiers on both sides and crystallizes so much of the war's mood that it deserves to be presented here.

It was written by Captain Ivar Campbell [10] from France during the winter of 1915.

The splutter of shrapnel, the red squeal of field guns, the growl of the heavies moving slowly through the air, the cr-r-r-ump of their explosion. But in a bombardment all tones mingle and their voice is like machinery running not smoothly but roughly, pantingly, angrily, wildly making shows of peace and wholeness.

You perceive, too, men infinitely small, running, affrighted rabbits, from the upheaval of shells, nerve-racked, deafened; clinging to earth, hiding eyes, whispering 'O God, O God!' You perceive, too, other men, sweaty, brown, infinitely small also, moving guns, feeding the belching monster, grimly, quietly pleased.

But with eyes looking over this land of innumerable eruptions you see no line. The land is inhuman.

But thousands of men are there; men who are below ground, men who have little bodies but immense brains. And the men facing West [the Germans] are saying, 'This is an attack, they will attack when this hell's over,' and they go on saying this to themselves continually.

And the men facing East [the British and French] are saying, 'We have got to get over the parapet. We have got to get over the parapet—when the guns lift.'

And then the guns lift up their heads and so a long, higher song.

And then untenanted land is suddenly alive with little men rushing, stumbling—rather foolishly leaping forward—laughing, shouting, crying in the charge.

There is one cheering thing. The men of the battalion— through all and in spite of that noisy, untasty day; through the wet cold night, hungry and tired, living now in mud and water, with every prospect of more rain tomorrow—are cheery. Sometimes, back in billets, I hate the men—their petty crimes, their continual bad language with no variety of expression, their stubborn moods. But in a difficult time they show up splendidly. Laughing in mud, joking in water—I'd 'demonstrate' [an army term for a tactical display of aggression] into Hell with some of them and not care.

9

Yet under shell-fire it was curious to look into their eyes—some of them little fellows from shops, civilians before, now and after: you perceived the wide, rather frightened, piteous wonder in their eyes, the patient look turned towards you, not, 'What the blankety, blankety hell *is* this?' but 'Is this quite fair? We cannot move, we are all little animals. Is it quite necessary to make such infernally large explosive shells to kill such infernally small and feeble animals as ourselves?'

I quite agreed with them, but had to put my eye-glass fairly in my eye and make jokes; and, looking back, I blush to think of the damnably bad jokes I did make!

Below are brief biographical details of the writers of the letters quoted in Chapter 1. They are listed here in the order in which their first letter appears.

1. *Gillespie*, Second-Lieutenant A. D., Argyll and Sutherland Highlanders. Born in Linlithgow, Scotland, Gillespie was educated at Winchester and Oxford and was reading for the Bar when he enlisted in August 1914. He was killed near La Bassée, 25 September, 1915, during the battle of Loos. His brother had been killed at the same place the previous October. (*See also* Chapter 2, pp. 12–15.)

2. *Henderson*, Keith. A capable artist, Henderson illustrated his letters to his wife, Helen. He finished the war as a captain in the Intelligence Corps, was awarded the O.B.E. and was twice mentioned in dispatches. Henderson was still living, aged eighty-eight, in 1972.

3. *Chapin*, Lance-Corporal Harold. Chapin was born in Brooklyn, U.S.A., on 15 February, 1886. His mother, an actress, brought her son to London when he was three. Educated at North London Collegiate School and afterwards at Norwich Grammar School, Chapin became an actor and then a playwright. Many of his plays, notably *Art and Opportunity*, *The Dumb and the Blind* and *It's the Poor that 'Elps the Poor*, were produced in London's West End. Happily married and with a three-year-old son he idolized, Chapin enlisted in the Royal Army Medical Corps from a sense of humanity. He was killed on 26 September, 1915, at the battle of Loos. (*See also* Chapter 4, pp. 30–3.)

4. *Bruhn,* Private Eduard. A student of theology. Born in Kiel, on 18 October, 1890. Bruhn was a student of theology before enlistment in the German Army. He was killed on 17 September, 1915, on the Russian front.

5. *Engall,* Second-Lieutenant John Sherwin. Born in 1896, Sherwin was educated at St Paul's School, London, and was to have gone to Cambridge but joined the 16th London Regiment. He was killed in action 1 July, 1916, while leading a platoon of his battalion's machine-gun company.

6. *Grenfell,* Captain the Hon. Julian Henry Francis. The son of Lord and Lady Desborough, Grenfell was born in 1888 and was educated at Eton and Oxford. He served in 1st Royal Dragoons, won the D.S.O. and died of wounds in France, 26 May, 1915. Grenfell wrote the well-known war poem *Into Battle.* His brother Gerald was killed 30 July, 1915.

7. *Garnett,* Lieutenant Kenneth Gordon. Born in 1893, Garnett was educated at St Paul's School, then Trinity College, Cambridge, where he was a Rowing Blue in 1914. Serving in the Royal Field Artillery, he won the M.C. and died of wounds received in action, France, 22 August, 1917.

8. The writer's name is not known; *see* Chapter 3.

9. *Wilson,* Captain Theodore Percival Cameron. Born in 1889, Wilson was educated at Oxford and became a schoolmaster and writer. While serving with the Sherwood Foresters, he was killed in action 23 March, 1918.

10. *Campbell,* Captain Ivar (*see also* Chapter 4, p. 37). Born in 1890, Campbell was educated at Eton and Christ Church, Oxford. A Scot, he served with the Argyll and Sutherland Highlanders and after a year on the Western Front, in France, was killed in Mesopotamia, 8 January, 1916.

2

*'A Grand Opportunity'** *

A. D. Gillespie.†   *1 October, 1914.*
To his parents.

We are just at the beginning of the struggle I'm afraid, and every hour we should remind ourselves that it is our great privilege to save the traditions of all the centuries behind us.

It's a grand opportunity, and we must spare no effort to use it, for if we fail we shall curse ourselves in bitterness every year that we live, and our children will despise our memory.

12 May, 1915.
From the trenches.

I have just been looking at a full-page photo in an illustrated weekly with the stirring title, 'How three encountered fifty and prevailed', and a footnote describing their gallant deeds in detail. The dauntless three belong to this regiment, but we were a little puzzled, because we have never been at La Bassée, where their exploit took place. A close inspection showed that the trees were in full leaf, and that the men were wearing spats and hose-tops, which we have long since abandoned for general use. Finally, someone recognized the sergeant as our shoemaker

---

* All chapter headings and headings within chapters are quotations from letters.

† Where no biographical details appear before a soldier's letter they will be found at the end of Chapter 1, his first letter having been quoted in that chapter.

12

sergeant, and his companions as two men from our second line transport. They are usually at least three miles from the trenches, and the whole story is a lie from beginning to end, without a shadow of truth in it. It makes one distrust all newspapers more than ever, to catch them out like that. The photo must have been taken somewhere on the retreat last year . . . [i.e. the retreat from Mons in August, 1914.]

30 July, 1915.
Billets.

. . . It's one disadvantage of our voluntary system that the press and every one else try to persuade officers and men that they are little heroes to have come out here at all, and that they deserve the best of everything: whereas they are just doing what every Frenchman has got to do as a matter of course. I'm for encouraging the men in a tight place, and for keeping them as busy as possible at all other times. There's just a bit too much sitting still, and not firing at the Germans because it will only make them fire back; but we should always fire when there is any target, and take jolly good care to aim straighter; it's the only way to end the war, and we know that when we take the trouble we can always give them more than we get.

The Russians seem to have checked the Germans for the time, but it will be a hard task to hold that salient with the Germans pressing in from three sides. I don't know more than anyone else why we are waiting so long for the next move on this front, but there must be some good reason.

Gillespie refers to the Polish-Galician salient. The Russian front collapsed early in August and by 19 September the Germans had advanced 300 miles. The 'good reason' for inactivity on the Western Front that summer was that the Allies had been exhausted by their costly and unsuccessful assaults.

I have been sleeping this afternoon, so far as the flies would let me, and listening in the intervals to flirtations in broken English, and still more broken French, between the men and the dairymaids at the farm. The French all seem to like les Ecossais [the Scottish soldiers] better than the English regiments; they come back to their houses sometimes if they hear a Scotch regiment is coming there.

I see Tom Erskine of the 4th Battalion is killed; he was one of the nicest of the Glasgow O.T.C. men, very competent and a keen soldier; his name was in the list with Eric Colbourne's for the Military Cross. That's the worst of this damnable war; it just lops off the bravest men as you might lop off the tallest heads of bracken with your stick, and once a man gets a reputation for keeping his head, and doing difficult jobs, he's bound to be picked for them. However it's a fine life out here, and if I come through I shall never regret the time spent in the trenches; one can't call them 'crowded hours' [a reference to Mordaunt's verse quoted by Sir Walter Scott in *Old Mortality*, 'One crowded hour of glorious life is worth an age without a name'] but they are as well spent as any in peace time.

24 September, 1915.
Trenches.

My dear Daddy,—This is your birthday, I think, but this trench has not provided me with a present.

We had an eight-mile march down last night, an extraordinary hot night, hotter than any I remember this summer. There was a lot of R.E. material—timber and so on—to carry up, and just as we reached the end of our mile-long communication trench, down came the rain. Of course in five minutes every one was wet through and up to the eyes in mud, and it was terrible work to carry these heavy timbers up in slippery darkness, with only the flashes of lightning to help. The thunder drowned the sound of the guns, which is saying a lot, for they have never ceased night and day lately, and there is a tremendous bombardment of the German trenches going on as I write.

We got everything up in the end and we are beginning to dry now . . . unfortunately, the men can light no fires in these trenches, it's too near the Germans, but they had a ration of rum this morning to cheer them up. Before long I think we shall be in the thick of it, for if we do attack, my company will be one of those in front, and I am likely to lead it; not because I have been specially chosen for that, but because someone must lead, and I have been with the company longest. I have no forebodings, for I feel that so many of my friends will charge by my side, and if a man's spirit may wander back at all, especially to the places where he is needed most, then Tom himself [his brother, killed in action] will be here to help me, and give me courage and resource and that cool head which will be needed most of all to make the attack a success. For I know it is just as bad to run into danger uselessly as to hang back when we should be pushing on. It will be a great fight, and even when I think of you, I would not wish to be out of this. You remember Wordsworth's 'Happy Warrior':

> Who if he be called upon to face
> Some awful moment to which heaven has joined
> Great issues, good or bad, for human kind,
> Is happy as a lover, and is attired
> With sudden brightness like a man inspired.

Well, I never could be all that a happy warrior should be, but it will please you to know that I am very happy, and whatever happens, you will remember that.

Well, anything one writes at a time like this seems futile, because the tongue of man can't say all that he feels—but I thought I would send this scribble with my love to you and Mother.

Always your loving
Bey.

The British Army attacked at Loos the next day and before the battle ended on 14 October suffered 60,000 casualties for minor gains; Gillespie was killed. He had with him a copy of Bunyan's *Pilgrim's Progress*, which was returned to his parents. They found the following passage marked: 'Then I entered into the Valley of the Shadow of Death, and had no light for almost half way through it. I thought I should have been killed there, and the sun rose, and I went through that which was behind with far more ease and quiet.'

'Kindliness is that part of the German character . . .'

Friedrich (Fidus) Sohnrey, student of Political Economy, Berlin: born 21 December, 1887, at Mollenden. Killed 8 November, 1914, near Clamency, France.

24 October, 1914.
In the Trenches near Clamency.

I go every day into the village here to see a family with six children. The father is in the war. The woman says he is a Reserve Dragoon. She innocently believes that he has not yet been under fire, but she has had no news for two months. She sheds tears when she tells me that and hears that we get letters from home every day. I get hot water there so as to have a good wash after four days' interval but I can't stop too long, as suspicious scratchings on the part of the children indicate undesirable house-mates.

One does feel sorry for these poor people who have hardly a stitch of underclothing to change into, not to speak of anything to eat—nothing left but potatoes, and the woman is always tearfully asking me how much longer she and her children will have to go on living like that. She is always lamenting over the war: 'C'est triste pour nous et pour vous.' She lays the blame for it on the English and curses them. It makes her very unhappy when I tell her that we are making preparations for the winter and shall probably spend the Christmas in the village. She just sobs helplessly. By way of thanks I leave her some bread and army biscuit, which the children fall upon with shouts of delight. The youngest is five months old. It is true that one cow has been left in the village, by order of the Area-Commandant, to supply milk for the babies, but even so that is little enough. On the second day I gave each of the children two sous. The woman was very much pleased and touched by my sympathy. She followed me to the door and assured me that her house was always 'à votre disposition'.

We all pity these poor people, who are clinging to the last remnants of their former happy existence, though in constant danger of seeing all their possessions burnt and smashed up by their own artillery, and I hardly think that a single one of our soldiers would treat them with anything but friendliness. Many of the men habitually give them some of their bread. The inhabitants of the place gather round our field-kitchens regularly to collect their tribute. So we are seeing to it that our enemies do not starve. Kindliness is probably that part of the German character from which it derives its greatness. 'It is the German soul, that makes a sick world whole'—and no doubt that means the German heart.

This letter was written at a time when the Allied public was being swamped with anti-German propaganda—German soldiers were raping French and Belgian women, bayoneting babies, cutting off children's hands and despoiling churches. Atrocities certainly occurred but they were by no means general. Many French people preferred to billet Germans rather than British or French troops.

'The Supreme Experience.'

Alan Seeger, an American, served with the French Foreign Legion, which was brought to France early in the war to act as shock troops. Seeger, educated at Harvard, was a sensitive poet; the London *Daily Telegraph*, reviewing his collection of poems, said, 'He belongs by birthright to the company of immortals.' He was killed during a charge at Belloy-en-Santerre, 4 July, 1916.

23 October, 1914.

To his Mother.

We are about seventeen kilometres southeast of Reims. I am sitting on the curbstone of a street at the edge of the town. The houses end abruptly and the yellow vineyards begin here. The view is broad and uninterrupted to the crest, ten kilometres or so across the valley. Between this and ourselves are the lines of the two armies. A fierce cannonading is going on continually, and I lift my eyes from the sheet at each report to see the puffs of smoke two or three miles off. The Germans have been firing salvos of four shots over a little village where the French batteries are stationed, shrapnel that burst in little puffs of white smoke; the French reply with explosive shells that raise columns of dust over the German lines. Half of our regiment have left already for the trenches. We may go tonight. We have made a march of about seventy-five kilometres in four days and are now on the front, ready to be called on at any moment. I am feeling fine, in my element, for I have always thirsted for this kind of thing, to be present always where the pulsations are liveliest. Every minute here is worth weeks of ordinary *experience*. How beautiful the view is here, over the sunny vineyards! And what a curious anomaly. On this slope the grape pickers are singing merrily at their work, on the other the batteries are roaring. Boom! Boom!

This will spoil one for any other kind of life. The yellow

afternoon sunlight is sloping gloriously across this beautiful valley of Champagne. I must mail this now. There is too much to be said and too little time to say it. . . .

18 June, 1915.

To his Mother.   *Magneux.*

Received your letters and clippings yesterday on the march. I am not thinking of anything else but the business in hand, and if I write, it is only to divert the tedium of the trenches and to get a little intellectual exercise of which one stands so much in need now. You must not be anxious about my not coming back. The chances are about ten to one that I will. But if I should not, you must be proud, like a Spartan mother, and feel that it is your contribution to the triumph of the cause whose righteousness you feel so keenly. Everybody should take part in this struggle which is to have so decisive an effect, not only on the nations engaged but on all humanity. If so large a part should fall to your share you would be in so far superior to other women and should be correspondingly proud. There would be nothing to regret, for I could not have done otherwise than what I did, and I think I could not have done better. Death is nothing terrible after all. It may mean something even more wonderful than life. It cannot possibly mean anything worse to the good soldier. So do not be unhappy, but no matter what happens walk with your head high and glory in your large share of whatever credit the world may give me. . . .

8 August, 1915.

To his Mother.

You must not delude yourself about any revolutions in Germany or an early termination of the war. Look upon my being here just as I do, that is, as its being a part of my career. I am not influenced by the foolish American ideas of 'success', which regard only the superficial and accidental meanings of the word—advancement, recognition, power, etc. The essence of success is in rigorously obeying one's best impulses and following those paths which conscience absolutely approves, and than which imagination can conceive none more desirable. Given my nature, I could not have done otherwise than I have done. Anything conceivable that I might have done had I not enlisted would have been less than what I am doing now, and anything that I may do after the war is over, if I survive, will be less too. I have always had the passion to play the biggest part within my reach and it is really in a sense a supreme success to be allowed to play this. If I do not come out, I will share the good fortune of those who disappear at the pinnacle of their careers. Come to love France and understand the almost unexampled nobility of the effort this admirable people is making, for that will be the surest way of your finding comfort for anything that I am ready to suffer in their cause.

I am glad to hear that Thwing has joined the English. I used to know him at Harvard. He refused to be content, no doubt, with lesser emotions while there are hours to be lived such as are being lived now by young men in Flanders and Champagne. It is all to his credit. There should really be no neutrals in a conflict like this, where there is not a people whose interests are not involved. To neutrals who have stomached what America has consented to stomach from Germany [e.g. the sinking of the *Lusitania*, 7 May, 1915] whose ideals are so opposite to hers— who in the event of a German victory would be so inevitably embroiled, the question he put to himself and so resolutely answered will become more and more pertinent.

4 June, 1916.

To his Godmother.

. . . I hardly think we shall be here much longer. I have a presentiment that we are soon going into action. The last rumour is that we are soon to go to Verdun to relieve the 2nd Moroccan division. That would be magnificent, wouldn't it? The long journey drawing nearer and nearer to that furnace, the distant cannonade, the approach through the congested rear of the battle-line full of dramatic scenes, the salutations of troops that have already fought, 'Bon courage, les gars!' and then our own début in some dashing affair. *Verdun nous manque.* [We miss Verdun.] I should really like to go there, for after the war I imagine Frenchmen will be divided into those who were at Verdun and those who were not. . . .

28 June, 1916.

To a Friend.

We go up to the attack tomorrow. This will probably be the biggest thing yet. We are to have the honour of marching in the first wave. No sacks, but two *musettes* [haversacks] toile de tente [groundsheet] slung over shoulder, plenty of cartridges, grenades, and baïonnette au canon [rifle and bayonet].

I will write you soon if I get through all right. If not, my only earthly care is for my poems. Add the ode I sent you and the three sonnets to my last volume and you will have *opera omnia quae existant* [all the extant work].

I am glad to be going in first wave. If you are in this thing at all it is best to be in to the limit. And this is the supreme experience.

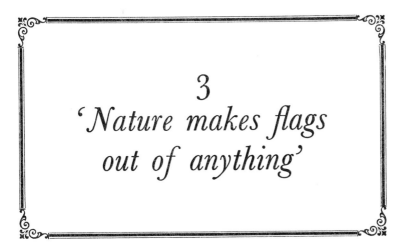

3
'Nature makes flags out of anything'

The writer of the following letters was a young French painter and junior officer who was at the front from August 1914 until he was posted missing in action in April 1915. His letters were published anonymously in 1917 and I have been unable to trace his name. In an introduction to the collection the English literary critic, A. C. Clutton-Brock, wrote, 'These letters reveal to us a new type of soldier, a new type of hero, almost a new type of man.' He meant that this soldier could endure without romantic illusions and had a steady faith without any formal revelation. 'His letters,' Clutton-Brock noted, 'are very French, that is to say, very unlike what any Englishman would write to his mother, or indeed to anyone.' He was referring, I think, to the emotional, poetic and philosophical nature of the letters.

14 November, 1914.

To his Mother.

Since half-past eight on the evening of the 12th we have been dragged about from place to place in the prospect of our taking part in a violent movement. We left at night, and in the calm of nature my thoughts cleared themselves a little, after the two days in billets during which one becomes a little too material. Our reinforcement went up by stealth. We awaited our orders in a barn, where we slept on the floor. Then we filed into the woods and fields, which the day, breaking through grey, red, and purple clouds, slowly lit up, in surroundings the most romantic and pathetic that could be imagined. In the full day-light of a charming morning we learnt that the troops ahead of us had inflicted enormous losses on the enemy [this rumour was false] and had even made a very slight advance. We then returned to our usual posts, and here I am again, beholding once more the splendour of the French country, so touching in this grey, windy, and impassioned November, with sunshine thrown in patches upon infinite horizons.

Dear mother, how beautiful it is, this region of spacious dignity, where all is noble and proportioned, where outlines are so beautifully defined!—the road bordered with trees diminish-ing towards the frontier, hills, and beyond them misty heights which one guesses to be the German Vosges. [The writer's unit was in the Verdun sector]. There is the scenery, and here is something better than the scenery. There is a Beethoven melody and a piece of Liszt called 'Bénédiction de Dieu dans la solitude'. Certainly we have no solitude, but if you turn the pages of Albert Samain's poems you will find an aphorism by Villiers de l'Isle-Adam: 'Know that there will always be solitude on earth for those who are worthy of it'. This solitude of soul that can ignore all that is not in tune with it. . . .

I have had two letters from you, of the 6th and 7th. Perhaps this evening I shall have another. Do not let us allow our courage to be concerned only with the waiting for letters from each other. But the letters are our life, they are what brings us our joys, our happiness, it is through them that we take delight in the sights of this world and of this time.

If your eyes are not strong, that is a reason for not writing, but apart from your health do not by depriving me of letters hold back your heart from me.

7 December, 1914.

My Beloved Mother,

I am writing this in the night . . . by six o'clock in the morning military life will be in full swing.

My candle is stuck on a bayonet, and every now and then a drop of water falls on to my nose. My poor companions try to light a reluctant fire. Our time in the trenches transforms us into lumps of mud.

The general good humour is admirable. However the men may long to return, they accept none the less heroically the vicissitudes of the situation. Their courage, infinitely less 'literary' than mine, is so much the more practical and adaptable; but each bird has its cry, and mine has never been a war-cry. I am happy to have felt myself responsive to all these blows, and my hope lies in the thought that they will have forged my soul. Also I place confidence in God and whatever He holds in store for me.

I seem to foresee my work in the future. Not that I build much on this presentiment, for all artists have conceived work which has never come to light. Mozart was about to make a new start when he died, and Beethoven planned the 'Tenth Symphony' in ignorance of the all too brief time that was to be allowed him by destiny.

It is the duty of the artist to open his flowers without dread of frost, and perhaps God will allow my efforts to fulfil themselves in the future. My very various attempts at work all have an indescribable immaturity about them still, a halting execution, which consorts badly with the real loftiness of the intention. It seems to me that my art will not quite expand until my life is further advanced. Let us pray that God will allow me to attain. . . .

As for what is in your heart, I have such confidence in your courage that this certainty is my great comfort in this hour. I know that my mother has gained that freedom of soul which allows contemplation of the universal scheme of things. I know from my own experience how intermittent is this wisdom, but even to taste of it is already to possess God. It is the security I derive from knowledge of your soul and your love, that enables me to think of the future in whatever form it may come.

23 January, 1915.

To his Mother.

. . . As for me, I have no desires left. When my trials are really hard to bear, I rest content with my own unhappiness, without facing other things.

When they become less hard, then I begin to think, to dream, and the past that is dear to me seems to have that same remote poetry which in happier days drew my thoughts to distant countries. A familiar street, or certain well-known corners, spring suddenly to my mind—just as in other days islands of dreams and legendary countries used to rise at the call of certain music and verse. But now there is no need of verse or music; the intensity of dear memories is enough.

I have not even any idea of what a new life could be. I only know that we are making life here and now.

For whom, and for what age? It hardly matters. What I do know, and what is affirmed in the very depths of my being, is that this harvest of French genius will be safely stored, and that the intellect of our race will not suffer for the deep cuts that have been made in it.

Who will say that the rough peasant, comrade of the fallen thinker, will not be the inheritor of his thoughts? No experience can falsify this magnificent intuition. The peasant's son who has witnessed the death of the young scholar or artist will perhaps take up the interrupted work, be perhaps a link in the chain of evolution which has been for a moment suspended. This is the real sacrifice: to renounce the hope of being the torch-bearer. To a child in a game it is a fine thing to carry the flag: but for a man, it is enough to know that the flag will yet be carried. And that is what every moment of great august Nature brings home to me. Every moment reassures my heart: Nature makes flags out of anything. They are more beautiful than those to which our little habits cling. And there will always be eyes to see and cherish the lessons of earth and sky.

22 February, 1915.

Dear Beloved Mother,   *(1st day in billet)*

I will tell you about the goodness of God, and the horror of these things. The heaviness of heart that weighed me down this month and a half past was for the coming anguish to be undergone.

We reached the scene of action on the 17th. The preparation ceased to interest me; I was all expectation of the event. It broke out at three o'clock: the explosion of seven mines under the enemy's trenches. It was like a distant thunder. Next, five hundred guns created the hell into which we leapt.

Night was coming on when we established ourselves in the positions we had taken. All that night I was actively at work for the security of our men, who had not suffered much. I had to cover great tracts, over which were scattered the wounded and the dead of both sides. My heart yearned over them, but I had nothing better than words to give them. In the morning we were driven, with serious loss, back to our previous positions, but in the evening we attacked again: we retook our whole advance; here again I did my duty. In my advance I got the sword of an officer who surrendered; after that I placed my men for guarding our ground. The captain ordered me to his side, and I gave him the plan of our position. He was telling me of his decision to have me mentioned, when he was killed before my eyes.

Briefly, under the frightful fire of those three days, I organized and kept going the work of supplying cartridges; in this job five of my men were wounded. Our losses are terrible; those of the enemy greater still. You cannot imagine, beloved mother, what man will do against man. For five days my shoes have been slippery with human brains, I have walked among lungs, among entrails. The men eat, what little they have to eat, at the side of the dead. Our regiment was heroic; we have no officers left. They all died as brave men. Two good friends—one of them a fine model of my own for one of my last pictures—are killed. That was one of the terrible incidents of the evening. A white body, splendid under the moon! I lay down near him. The beauty of things awoke again for me.

At last, after five days of horror that lost us twelve hundred men, we were ordered back from the scene of abomination.

The regiment has been mentioned in despatches.

Dear mother, how shall I ever speak of the unspeakable things I have had to see? But how shall I ever tell of the certainties this tempest has made clear to me? Duty; effort.

The writer had lived through a series of unsuccessful French attacks in the area between Reims and Verdun. Between 1 January and 30 March the French suffered 400,000 casualties in the fighting, a continuation of the first Battle of Champagne.

5 March, 1915.
Billets.

To his Mother.

I wish I could recover in myself the extreme sensibilities I felt before the fiery trial, so that I might describe for you the colours and the aspects of the drama we have passed through. But just now I am in a state of numbness, pleasant enough in

itself, yet apt to hinder my vision of things present and my fore-
casts of things to come. I have to make an effort to keep hold of
eternal and essential things; perhaps I shall succeed in time.

And yet certain sights on the wasted field of war had so noble
a lesson, a teaching so persuasive, that I should love to share
with you the great certainties of those days. How harmonious is
death within the natural soil, how admirable is the manner of
man's return to the substance of his mother earth, compared
with the poverty of funeral ceremonial! Yesterday I thought of
those poor dead as forsaken things. But I had been present at the
burial of an officer, and it seems to me that Nature is more
compassionate than man. Yes indeed, the soldier's death is
close to natural things. It is a frank horror, a horror that does
not attempt to cheat the law of violence. I often passed close to
bodies that were gradually passing into the clay, and their
change seemed more comforting than the cold and unchanging
aspect of the tombs of town cemeteries. From our life in the
open we have gained a freedom of conception, an amplitude of
thought and of habit, which will for ever make cities horrible
and artificial to those who survive the war.

Dear mother, I write but ill of things that I have greatly felt.
Let us seek refuge in the peace of spring and in the treasure of
the present moment.

The writer sent his last letter on 6 April, the day on which the
Battle of Woëvre began. Repeated French assaults against the
north face of the St.-Mihiel salient were repulsed with heavy
losses. This sensitive French painter disappeared early in the
action—probably blown to pieces.

'If only I might give my life for our Germany.'

Walter Roy, born 1 June, 1894, in Hamburg, was a student of
medicine at Jena before enlistment. He was killed in the attack
on the Heights of Combres near Les Eparges on 24 April, 1915.

14 November, 1914.

To his Sweetheart. *Döberitz.*

. . . Oh how suddenly everything has changed! First the free,
sunshiny, enchanting summer, golden happiness, a life of

liberty, enthusiasm for Nature, poetry, music, brightness and joy, all the effervescence of youth: oh, what a lovely summer it was! And now cold, cruel, bitter earnest, stormy winter, death and misery! And everything vanished so suddenly. How I lived and loved is now like a dream, a passing mood, the sweet remembrance of a passing mood. Only one thing is real now—the war! And the only thing that now inspires and uplifts one is love for the German Fatherland and the desire to fight and risk all for Emperor and Empire. All else is thrust into the background and is like a dream, like a distant rosy cloud in the evening sky.

When, on the march, I observed the autumn beauties of Nature, then indeed I thought sadly and yearningly: I should like to dream about you, to love you, to sing of you, to be rapt and meditative, but I have no time for you now: I am entirely occupied with thoughts of war and suffering and with enthusiasm for our holiest duty. Lenau, Goethe, Eichendorff, Schwind and Feuerbach, Beethoven, Wagner, Puccini, and Mozart—how I long for them! But I could not really enjoy them now, I could not live in their spirit. Thoughts press in upon me, so many, so urgent, but I can't think them. I lack the needful repose and quiet.

I sometimes think that I have become rather strange. But when at last, at long last, I get to the Front—it should be about December—then if only I might give my life for our Germany, for my Kaiser, for my Fatherland! I have had a life, short indeed, but so beautiful, so golden, so full of light and warmth, that I should be happy to die if I had only myself to consider. And this life full of light and sunshine I owe to the dear people whose thoughts accompany me and of whom you too are one.

Roy seems to have had a premonition of death and wrote a last note to his family before going into battle. '. . . This is going to be a terrible battle and it is radiant, enchanting springtime! . . . If I am to die I shall do so joyfully, gratefully and happily! . . .'

' *The English didn't want to shoot any more* '

Karl Aldag was born on 26 January, 1889, at Oberkirchen, and became a student of philosophy at Marburg University. He was killed on 15 January, 1915, near Fromelles. Deeply religious, Aldag wrote to his family at Christmas, 1914, 'I wish you all a devout, holy Christmas Feast, which will bring happiness and joy into the house, and trust in the God of Love who will protect us all.' In the following letter he expresses the belief commonly held by German soldiers that British politicians were entirely responsible for the war.

3 January, 1915.

To a Friend.

I have lit a pipe and settled myself at the table in our cow-house in order to write home, where they are certainly looking for news again.

New Year's Eve was very queer here. An English officer came across with a white flag and asked for a truce from 11 o'clock till 3 to bury the dead; just before Christmas there were some fearful enemy attacks here in which the English lost many in killed and prisoners. The truce was granted. It is good not to see the corpses lying out in front of us any more. The truce was moreover extended. The English came out of their trenches into no-man's land and exchanged cigarettes, tinned-meat and photographs with our men, and said they didn't want to shoot any more. So there is an extraordinary hush, which seems quite uncanny. Our men and theirs are standing up on the parapet above the trenches. . . .

That couldn't go on indefinitely, so we sent across to say that they must get back into their trenches as we were going to start firing. The officers answered that they were sorry, but their men wouldn't obey orders. They didn't want to go on. The soldiers said they had had enough of lying in wet trenches, and that France was done for.

They are really much dirtier than we are, have more water in their trenches and more sick. Of course they are only mercenaries, and so they are simply going on strike. Naturally we didn't shoot either, for our communication trench leading from the village to the firing-line is always full of water, so we are very glad to be able to walk on the top without any risk. Suppose the whole English army strikes, and forces the gentlemen in London to chuck the whole business! Our lieutenants went over and wrote their names in an album belonging to the English officers.

Then an English officer came across and said that the Higher Command had given orders to fire on our trench and that our men must take cover, and the French artillery began to fire, certainly with great violence but without inflicting any casualties.

We called across to tell each other the time and agreed to fire a salvo at 12. It was a cold night. We sang songs, and they clapped (we were only 60–70 yards apart); we played the mouth-organ and they sang and we clapped. Then I asked if they hadn't got any musical instruments, and they produced some bagpipes (they are the Scots Guards, with the short petticoats and bare legs) [one brigade of the 7th Division, which was holding the British line at this point, consisted of Grenadier Guards, Scots Guards and Gordon Highlanders, which may have given rise to the mistaken idea that the Scots Guards were a kilted regiment] and they played some of their beautiful elegies on them, and sang, too. Then at 12 we all fired salvoes *into the air*!

Then there were a few shots from our guns (I don't know what they were firing at) and Verey lights crackled like fireworks, and we waved torches and cheered. We had brewed some grog and drank the toast of the Kaiser and the New Year.

4
'Oh Lord, the mystery of men's feelings'

Harold Chapin (*see* Chapter 1, p 10).

30 March, 1915.

To his Son, aged three.   *France.*

Hullo Vallie! I'm in France at the war at last. How are you? We are having such a funny time all sleeping on straw on the floor—think of that when you get into your little cribble-cot tonight.

I am sitting writing this on a sack on the ground with my back against Jack's. You remember Jack the cook? In front of me are all the horses in rows and rows tied to pegs driven into the ground. They are tied by the head—the way Modestine used to be—to one peg and by the hind foot to another peg to prevent them turning round and kicking each other. They don't like having their hind foots [*sic*] tied and pull at them and swear with their ears. They try to kick too, just as she used to do.

There are soldiers all about here all busy shoving the Germans back and *shoving* the Germans back and SHOVING the Germans back, and sooner or later we shall shove the whole lot of them right back into Germany over the Rhine—which is a big river—bigger than the river at Maidenhead—RIGHT back into Germany and off their feet, and then we shall sit on their heads severely until they have had enough, and then the war will be over, and we shall just have to tidy up and come home and I shall come home to you my Darling and the Blessed Mummy and the nice flat at St. John's Wood, and Oh,

I do hope it will be soon because I want to see you and Mummy most awfully.

Goodbye my precious, please give my love to Gram and tell her I wish I could have some English Turkey. And please Vallie send everybody you can out here to help shove, because the sooner the Germans are shoved over and the more of us there are to sit on their heads, the sooner I shall see you all again.

Your Doody.

4 May, 1915.

To his Wife.

This is a week of sensations but I really think last night will be unbeaten at the end of the war. It was by moonlight—almost full—that adds something, don't you think? I had taken three men in answer to a message incoherently delivered by a man on horseback, accompanied by two cyclists—

'Man gone mad down at —— They've got 'im in a little room by the railway station.'

We found him not raving but apparently asleep, wrapped in blankets quiet as death. A stretcher was brought out of the motor and about a dozen spare stretcher slings I had thought to bring—fortunately—and we debated a moment in the moonlight. What a curious group we must have been on the deserted station platform, standing round him! Then one of his chums touched him. You must imagine more than I can describe in this chatter. He raved and bit and beat out with fists and feet snarling like a dog—*really like* a dog—we got him on to a stretcher, and I lashed him on as gently as I could but very firmly. Once bending across him I touched his face with my sleeve, he had it in his teeth in a minute—and in the midst of it men passed going up to the trenches singing. They passed along the road not fifty yards away while a dozen of us held him down by arms and legs and hair, and muffled him in blankets and packed him off with two of our men and two of his chums to our snug little brand new hospital. Ashcroft [a medical orderly] and I then set out to walk in the moonlight with the star shells on the horizon [the second battle of Ypres was in progress] and the rattling line towards which we were walking (the station lies away from the firing line from here) that provided *the* sensation. I was naturally impressed. Ashcroft is a good obvious fellow. He prattled wonderingly of 'Wot would make a chap go off like that?' He supposed he had been 'too daring like' and it had '*told* on him'. 'These Engineers go mad very easy—' etc. Can't you hear him—an old liner steward—a bit of a gardener —a silk-hat maker last job—age about forty? The sort of man you meet fifty of in an hour.

We had to pass the wooded garden of the Chateau. In the wood are about two score graves, half of our men and half of Indians—beautifully tended graves shining in bead wreaths and pine crosses. Over them in the moonlight a nightingale was singing loud and sweet. Its first notes were so close and so low that I was startled.

Have I mentioned the spy we saw in uniform, being marched away under armed guard—swaggering but unable to swagger in a straight line. I shouldn't be surprised to hear he was no spy and got off—but he swaggered and he was frightened. That was what I saw.

I went up to H.Q. this afternoon and saw two men buried. Their chums were so particular to dig them a *level* grave and a *rectangular* grave and *parallel* graves, and to note who was in this grave, who in that, that my mind, jumping to questions as always, was aching with whys which I wouldn't have asked for the world—almost as if the answer—you take me—would disgrace me for not knowing it already, brand me as lacking some decency the grave-diggers had.

O Lord, the mystery of men's feelings.

1 September, 1915.

To his Wife.

Thanks very much for your latest just received. This letter may be broken off at any moment and I shall post it at once. We are waiting for the whistle to toot, fall in, and start packing our waggons for a move—quite an unimportant one as far as we know, not up to the line. I shan't be sorry to leave this part of France—it is decidedly damp—night mists and unlimited dew in addition to getting all the rain of the neighbourhood and I am rather rheumaticky again. Not acutely by any means, just stiff joints and hard lumps in the muscles in the mornings.

Don't encourage Vallie to talk about God, there's a dear. It really troubles me very much to think that he's having his little mind, even slightly, swayed by . . .

Letters from the Front

Later.

I can't remember how I meant to finish above. My meaning is:—tell him all the fairy tales or nonsense stories you please but about God and religious subjects only tell him what you yourself unfeignedly believe to be true: if nothing, tell him nothing. I want him—as I did—to find a definite religious or philosophical *attitude* (which means more, really, than a credo) towards what he sees—what he thinks he should do—what he fails to understand—*for himself*. One cannot learn an attitude or acquire it from others—it is at best a pose. One must make it for oneself, and by giving a child an idea that the cosmos is a sort of toy shop run by a tyrant (tyrants could be benevolent—don't misunderstand the term) with a curious hobby—the rewarding of certain acts and the punishment of others and the forgiveness of certain of the latter acts as a reward for 'repentance' coupled with a belief in the tyrant's existence—to teach a child this is to give it an altogether unreal cosmos to face and adapt his attitude to and build to.

Fairy tales are quite different. They are confessed imaginings: not told as authoritatives—at least by intelligent people.

Ring off.

Love.

Chapin wrote his last letter on 24 September, 1915. He told his wife:

This is my ideal of happiness (under war conditions)—to arrive back after a hard day's navvying among nice big bangs (I really do like the noise of guns—unhealthy taste, eh?) to come back to camp and tea healthily tired *and* find a letter from you waiting for me. . . .

' It makes me grin '

Lieutenant Denis Oliver Barnett was educated at St Paul's School and was scholar-elect of Balliol College, Oxford. Joining the Army on leaving school, he was posted to the Leinster Regiment, British Army, and killed in action, Flanders, 15 August, 1915, during a raid on German trenches. He was twenty years of age.

19 May, 1915.
Billets.

To his Father.

You are one of God's own dears. Thank you very much for your photograph, which I like very much.

I've got a long account to settle out here, and Kenneth [his best friend] is at the top of it. I think they'll find that will cost them a lot. His death hits me harder than the death of all the valiant men I've grown to like and love out here.

The love that grows quickly and perhaps artificially when men are together up against life and death has a peculiar quality. Death that cuts it off does not touch the emotions at all, but works right in the soul of you; this is so incomprehensible that you are only vaguely conscious of the change which you find there later, and shake hands with it. Regret is what you feel; but there is something rather better than that really, which I think is what makes men.

Don't be anxious about chlorine—we've got it beaten by an extraordinary rapidity of organization which is quite unlike the work of the Army I belong to.

I do hope you aren't having a θυμοφθόρος [soul-destroying] time at inspections. I'm always thinking about you and praying that you aren't unhappy about me or any other worry. If there is any soul ευδαίμων [blessed] in this world, it is me—real happiness of the whole being, the only sort there is, οὖσα ευδαιμονία [real happiness]. It makes me sing and grin to myself in the dark. And thank God, I believe I can do what is up to me.

The chlorine to which Barnett refers was the first use of poison gas on the Western Front. The Germans spread it from 5,000 cylinders during a surprise attack on 22 April, which heralded the beginning of the second battle of Ypres. It was an error of judgment: the prevailing winds in France are westerlies so that the Germans were bound to suffer more from gas than the Allies, who were quick to retaliate with it.

'England is too much of a gentlemen'

Henry Bentinck was born (1881) into an upper-class English family which prized the military and religious virtues. Educated at Harrow, Bentinck went to Trinity College, Cambridge, where he took a degree in Law. A superb sportsman and athlete, he joined the Army and was attached to his father's old regiment, the Coldstream Guards, serving for a time in Egypt and the Sudan. He was noted in his regiment as 'a Christian gentleman'. Once, when asked his opinion about moral standards, he replied, 'My standard is fixed by the regulations of my commanding officer, and my commanding officer is Jesus Christ.' A captain in 1912, he was mentioned in despatches in December 1915 and was promoted to major in January 1916. He suffered multiple wounds in an advance from Guinchy, 15 September, 1916, and died on 2 October. He was unmarried and most of his letters were to his mother.

11 July, 1915.

My Darling Mama,

Sometimes one wonders why God allows iniquity (i.e. Germany) to apparently triumph so long and defers victory to us, when they stand for all that is wrong and unjust and we stand for all that is right and just, but then if God deals with a nation as with an individual we know that whom He loveth He chasteneth, etc., and that England with all her faults, which are many, has and does stand for justice and freedom. Can you imagine anything more intolerable than a Europe under Germany's thumb?

13 October, 1915.

My Darling Mama,

I am interested to see Sir John French's account of the Hun attack of the 8th, and of his mention of the trench which was re-won by our 3rd Battalion bombers, though he does not mention the units. There *are* gentlemen even amongst the Huns. Two wounded Grenadiers crawled back into the lines the other day; they had been lying out for five days near the German trenches and said that every night a German officer used to bring them coffee and cigarettes. He said if they came into their lines the Huns would kill them, but he was not going to prevent them getting back to our lines if they could.

35

20 March, 1916.

To his Mother.

I quite agree with you that it is merely an insult and the greatest at that, to compare England with the Huns. England has one great fault which friend and foe mostly realize, and though no doubt it costs us much at times I must say I glory in it—that is, that England is too much of a gentleman in war and in diplomacy; we have often made the fatal mistake of judging others by our own standards.

I often think it is quite pathetic that so many gallant Hun privates should be sacrificed for *such* a cause and for *such* leaders. . . .

The Divisional artillery had a horse-show the other day when we were out and I judged most of the classes. I rode my C.O.'s horse in the jumping competition and won handsomely from a field of twenty-five. It was in the snow and they had put down straw to jump from.

I love your news of old Vike [a family friend] and I love hearing about the children, give them and Vike all my love. I love Alec knowing all the pigeons by their faces. If he doesn't want to shoot why should he? So long as he is brave that is the only thing really that matters as far as manliness is concerned. . . .

23 April, 1916.

Addressee unknown.

I loved your fierce patriotism. I always think England is like a man who is blessed or cursed with a conscience and who is continually doing stupid things because he is so afraid of doing the wrong thing and it rather hinders him taking strong action.

11 May, 1916.

My Darling M——.

There is a charming wood behind my trenches though much battered about. I have to go through it to join up with my other half company and generally contrive to find myself in it at 3 a.m. when it is glorious. The ground is covered with wild flowers—marsh marigolds and flowers that look like mignonette but which aren't. It also has wood pigeons, cuckoos, small birds, and an occasional rabbit, which makes me wish for a pack of beagles whose music would astonish the Hun. My company has found? A ferret! Why should it take ten years off your life if A got a staff job and you felt he was out of the trenches and

firing line. I admire your fierce patriotism which would place
him in the forefront of the battle, but hardly expected it would
kill you if he didn't get there!!

It has often been said that upper-class women drove their men
to the war; the attitude of the woman to whom Bentinck was
writing gives point to the premise. Many women would have
nothing to do with an officer not serving with a trench battalion.

'For these things are natural'

Bentinck's observations about nature and the war were super-
ficial compared with those of Captain Ivar Campbell (*see*
Chapter 1) writing from France about the same time as
Bentinck. He wrote with competence and compassion.

Addressee unknown.

. . . It is difficult to write things out here. Journalists do it, yet
miss the note of naturalness which strikes me. For these things are
natural. I suppose we have been fighting a thousand thousand
years to a thousand years' peace; they miss, too, the beauty of the
scene and action as a whole—that beauty defined as something
strange, rarefied; our deep passions made lawful and evident;
our desires made acceptable; our direction straight. Such will
be the impressions to linger, to be handed on to future generations, as the Napoleonic wars are fine adventures for us. Here,
present and glaring to our eyes in trenches and billets, the more
abiding and deeper meanings of the war are readable.

Here is the scene I shall remember always: A misty summer
morning—I went along to a sap-head running towards the
German line at right angles to our own. Looking out over the
country, flat and uninteresting in peace, I beheld what at first
would seem to be a land ploughed by the ploughs of giants. . . .
Trenches rise up, grey clay, three or four feet above the ground.
Save for one or two men—snipers—at the sap-head, the
country was deserted. No sign of humanity—a dead land . . .
there was no sound but a cuckoo in a shell-torn poplar. Then,
as a rabbit in the early morning comes out to crop grass, a
German stepped over the enemy trench—the only living thing
in sight. 'I'll take him,' says the man near me. And like a rabbit
the German falls. And again complete silence and desolation. . . .

5
'An extraordinary elation'

Lieutenant John Hugh Allen, a New Zealander, was educated at Wanganui College and then travelled to England to read Law at Jesus College, Cambridge. He joined the Worcestershire Regiment, British Army, and was killed in action on Gallipoli, 6 June, 1915, at the age of twenty-eight. This letter was written six days before his death.

A Base (Gallipoli) 31 May, 1915.

To All at Arana and Wairewa [his family],

This is happiness! We reached this base between 2 and 4 this morning. All yesterday we were in a second-line trench. Our relief was to come at 9 p.m. We took our places shortly before, and were under heavy rifle fire, and the trench was in parts enfiladable [open to fire along its length from the flank]. The regiment before us lost several men in the trench for this reason. 9, 10, 11, 12 passed, and no relief came—our hearts sank. Then a messenger passed through the trench saying: 'You'll get no relief tonight.' Immediately after the relief came!

We filed away through trench after trench, and occasionally doubled over open country. Soldiers asleep in every imaginable position—below their overcoats one saw mud-stained putties and boots. The young sentry said: 'This shrapnel is awful', as though it could be prevented, and in the name of reason it should be stopped. Then we got into a deep nullah, and gradually the sound of rifle fire took softer and softer tones.

38

The perfect moon is still with us, and the temperature of the night was delightful.

I felt an extraordinary elation. It was not so much that one had left the firing-line as that one had been in it. I often think of H. Benson's story of the man who knew he was to be tortured and of the agony of his dread. When he was put on the wheel they saw he smiled. His suffering was less than his suspense. Full of wretchedness and suspense as the last few days have been, I have enjoyed them. They have been intensely interesting. They have been wonderfully inspiring.

That they have been so is due to the men with whom I have been.

It has been heart-breaking seeing men one had got to like only in a day or so killed—or worse, receive wounds of which they died. It has been bad enough for me. It is unspeakably worse for those who had been their soldier friends, who have drilled, slept, eaten, worked, and now died together. The men have been twelve days in the trenches and are shaken in morale. A groaning, tortured man lying below you in a trench is not pleasant company. Three days and nights we have been at work almost continuously. Yesterday we had a quiet day after we left the fire trench. The men talked about wounds and dead men all day. It was getting on their nerves—remember Wellington's observation that every man in uniform is not a hero. When a man is hit, their way of putting it is that he has ceased to reign —so many kingdoms of this sort have been shattered lately. . . .

'As game as a pebble'

Major Oliver Hogue was born at Darlington, New South Wales, 29 April, 1880, and was a journalist before joining the 14 Australian Light Horse Regiment as an ordinary trooper. He became known as 'Trooper Bluegum', under which pseudonym he published (Andrew Melrose, London, 1916) his *Love Letters of an Anzac*. (A.N.Z.A.C. = Australian and New Zealand Army Corps.) His style was bright, brash and confident—qualities typical of Australian soldiers of the time. He signed his letters variously 'Jim Bluegum', 'Your khaki Lover', 'Yours till death, Corporal J.B.' Hogue's letter shows the spirit with which the Diggers fought at Gallipoli, and their ready acceptance of anti-German propaganda. Always enthusiastic in his soldiering, Hogue became staff officer to an Australian general. He died on 3 March, 1919, during the influenza epidemic which swept the world.

3 August, 1915.

My Bonnie Jean,   *Ryrie's Post, Anzac.*

You'll be sorry to hear that poor Harry Robson is dead, killed on 24 July by a shrapnel shell. He was one of the patriots, well off, with a wife and family, automobile and everything that makes life worth living. Yet when Britain stepped in to defend Belgium and when Australia offered 20,000 men, Lieutenant Robson heard the Empire call and buckled on his sword. (By the bye, Australia will have sent nearly 250,000 men to the war soon.)

Robson was all over South Africa with Colonel Cox during the South African War and was a splendid transport officer. He could do anything with horses and cattle. On various occasions when the columns were stuck up and bogged in the drifts he managed to improvise some scheme for getting the wagons through. He was a great swordsman and won several prizes at the big tournaments when he went to London with the New South Wales Lancers. We put up a cross with crossed swords over the little shallow grave on Shell Green. May poor old Robbo rest in peace!

Tresilian has gone—top-sergeant Tresilian, whom you met at the camp. He was reckoned quite the best of all the non-coms in our regiment and was generally looked upon as certain for a commission. He was game as a pebble, a regular dare-devil, and he never knew what fear was. He came from down Wagga way originally, but of late had been a station manager in the north-west of New South Wales. He got a bullet in his brain, when looking over the parapet on Holly Ridge, and died without a sound.

Did I tell you about Major Midgley? He is one of the very best officers in our brigade, got the D.S.O. in the Zulu War, went through the South African War, and is a regular little fire-eater. He is in charge of Chatham's Post and is always pulling the Turks' leg. He conceives the most wonderful ruses and tricks to worry the Turks and draw their fire. He sends out fiery arrows and rockets and flares, and by simulating preparations for attack at all times, he has the Turks in the Gaba Tepe zone worried to death.

The other night, however, one of his patrols nearly got cut off. They went out under Lieutenant Bolingbroke to try and snare a prisoner, but as they went south along the beach a strong Turkish patrol tried to sneak in behind them and cut them off from our lines. Our lads streaked back like startled wallabies. The men on the post could not give covering fire for fear of hitting our patrol. However, they all got back safely, and the moment they were in, Chatham's Post opened a hot fire and sent the venturesome patrol about their business. They must have thought that the Post was only lightly held, for some time after midnight a couple of hundred Turks made a dash at the Beach Post. They gave us warning by accidentally kicking the tins we had scattered in the grass. Our chaps were ready and the first Turkish shot was answered by a veritable fusillade from our lines, and after a half-hour's hot firing the enemy drew off.

We have come to the conclusion here that only about 10 per cent of the Turks are good shots and snipers, while about 90 per cent of the Light Horsemen are crack marksmen. This being so, we are able to keep their snipers well in subjection. Lately in front of Ryrie's Post and Chatham's, the Turks cannot show a periscope without having it smashed, and our lads now are actually shooting them through their loopholes and smashing the mud bricks with which the Turks surround their fire recesses.

Several of our snipers are putting up fine records in the matter of bagging Turks. But the champion sniper of them all is Trooper Sing of the 5th Light Horse. He is a champion shot, terrible quick on the up-take (as your mither would say), has keen eyesight, and abundant patience. He has now shot over one hundred Turks; and every one is vouched for by an officer or the sergeant on duty, who sits by Sing all day with a telescope and never gives him credit for a kill unless he actually sees the Turk fall. Some of the infantry on our left are rather inclined to be sceptical as to Sing's performances, but there is not the slightest doubt about it. Major Midgley reckons that Sing must have killed at least one hundred and twenty and wounded thirty more, but he only gives credit for those the observer sees actually fall. But Sing never shoots at a stretcher-bearer. He will wait for hours for a sniper. 'There is always tomorrow,' he says.

Our sharpshooters always get a bag when a batch of Turkish reinforcements arrive. The newcomers don't know the ropes.

They are always very inquisitive, and will go poking their heads up over the parapets, or round sandbags. They don't know that while they may not be visible in front they are 'wide open' from either flank, and with trenches rather zigzagging here and there, well, as Sing says, 'It's a shame to take the money.' One old Turk yesterday was fixing his overhead cover, when one of the Fifth smashed a brick and the thing toppled down on top of him. He lay quite exposed, kicking and yelling and waving his arms frantically. Sing exclaimed, 'I'll put the poor cuss out of his agony', and promptly put a bullet through his brain.

Doesn't all this sound shockingly cruel and callous, my darling? But you made me promise to tell you everything; anyhow I have broken my promise time and time again. I simply can't tell you about the aftermath of battle—the shockingly mangled bodies and the comrades maimed and crippled, and the agonies of those poor wounded fellows left between the two firing lines. Yet we are all erring mortals, when we try to gloss over the horrors of war. It's only when the women of the world realize all war's wickedness and misery that there will be even a faint chance of turning our swords into ploughshares. . . . Yet I remember when poor Belgium was trodden beneath the iron heel of the Hun, her shrines desecrated, her citizens butchered and her women outraged, it was the women of Great Britain that gladly sent their men to avenge the wrongs of the plucky little kingdom. And when the Empire called, the women of Australia gladly bade their sons and brothers 'Go and God-speed'. You, too, are not blameless in this regard, my angel, for if you had lifted your little finger to hold me back, I would have been numbered amongst the shirkers. . . .

When will it all end, I wonder? How long, O Lord, how long? Yet I know we cannot sheathe the sword till the Hun is humbled and the spirit of Prussian Militarism quenched for good and all. As for the poor turbaned and malignant Turk, he's merely the unhappy dupe of the German intriguers. Our Australians don't hate the Turk like they do the Hun. The Turkish prisoners have taken quite a liking to the Australians—but they all voice their fear of the Australian bayonets. They call us the 'White Gurkhas'.

I'm getting long-winded today. Au revoir.

Yours ever,
J.B.

Letters from the Front

' Those men are very rare who think of their neighbours'

The Australians, New Zealanders and British are apt to forget
that French troops also served at Gallipoli. One of them was
Major Joseph de Grouchy, a doctor with Le Corps Expéditionnaire d'Orient. He wrote frequently to his English wife,
who often annoyed him by her desire to go to the war on her
own account.

19 July, 1915.

You tell me you are writing to Dr. R. Let me tell you that I do
not approve, and that I don't want you to leave Europe with a
war mission. I am absolutely put out and annoyed. I don't
understand where you get such ideas. There are enough men to
support the horrors of war without adding women. You say you
want to serve on a boat, but I hope they will only take very
experienced nurses. Others are useless and consequently harmful.

From an egotistical and personal point of view I could not,
without great anxiety and agitation, see you exposed to grave
dangers. I cannot even bear the thought of it. There are
enough fighters in your family and mine. And then imagine
that one day I might arrive ill or wounded at Toulon or
Marseilles. You would be gone!

If you came out on a hospital boat here I could not even go
and see you. I have not yet been on a single boat since I left the
Savoie on 29 April. I do not know how you picture our life here.
I beg of you to keep quiet, I am excessively annoyed at what
you are trying to do. But let us both forget this mad project.

I often thank you for my admirable watch. I had it attended
to in Alexandria, and since then it has not failed me. It does its
duty. You don't know how attached we become to our small
possessions, and how grateful we are to them for services
rendered.

As for people, it is incredible what diversities they exhibit in
situations like those here. Each has his egoism and his idiosyn-
crasies. Those men are very rare who, in impending danger and
in the face of death, think of their neighbours. The life in common, the emotions experienced, centred around the same
menace, throw into relief each one's qualities and defects.

It is seldom that this continuity does not conduce to indul-
gence, and render sympathetic the greater part of one's

'comrades'. Brave men are legion. The Service de Santé of the 6th [his own unit] is one family.

I was very stern at first. Now all goes smoothly. My ideas and my method of procedure are now known. I like my subordinates, and I think that many of them like me. They welcomed me so heartily when I returned to them. You should have seen the large handshakes of the blacks, with their frank, sonorous laughs.

As to the Europeans, I have some exceptional men. Sergeant Lamendier Afrighi is a Corsican, energetic, very brave, very clear-headed, who preferred to forgo promotion rather than leave me. The corporal stretcher-bearer is the priest who figures in my photographs of the mass. He is a silent fellow, with a very high idea of duty, ready for the most perilous and arduous missions, an example to everyone.

Yesterday, after visiting the sick, he said to me, 'It is Sunday. Can I say mass?' And under the casemate he made liturgical gestures. We stood behind him, following the service, and at the same time letting our imaginations wander. We could see beyond, the road whereon the men followed close on each other in a whirlwind of thick dust.

Farther on the vision took in the excavations of Eleonte, where other civilizations and other gods had had their actors, warriors, priests, and philosophers. Is there really today more beauty, more human pity?

But I forget the others. There is Corporal Riffat, who has been my secretary from the first, and who is remarkably capable. Of a very even temperament, he does his work with a smile. He was a clerk in the Banque de France, very refined, very intelligent, and well educated. There is the celebrated Borella, who is a cyclist. Never tired, of perfect temper, he carries a note as well in the midst of bullets and shrapnel as (formerly) in fields of poppies or (today) in gulfs of dust. He is a working electrician, and very clever.

You already know Korka—very clean, very lazy, thin, tall, knowing well how to put up a tent, a bed, but quite incapable of boiling an egg. Clerc, my groom, is a pearl. He is excellent, calm, clean, gentle. He looks after my horses to perfection. I ride every day. My 'Golden' is most beautiful, and I love him very much. But no one in the world so much as you, my wife.

Your Joe.

Major de Grouchy was Gallic to the end of his last letter from
the Dardanelles, written on 31 January, 1916. 'Goodbye,
goodbye, dearest one. Thousands and thousands of kisses,
without counting the real ones you are soon to have from
Your Impatient Lover.'

'*A good strong dose of Winston Churchill*'

Lieutenant Arthur George Heath, born in London 8 October,
1887, was educated at the Grocers' Company's School and in
1905 went to New College, Oxford, as Open Classical Scholar.
A true intellectual, he was elected a Fellow of the College in
1909, a measure of his brilliance. He lectured mostly on modern
philosophy and gave much of his time to the Workers' Educational Association, then embryonic. A profound sense of duty
and idealism took him into the Army—as a lieutenant in the
6th Battalion, Royal West Kent Regiment, British Army. He
died, shot through the neck, on 8 October, 1915—his twenty-
eighth birthday. This calm, dispassionate letter gives an
honest impression of life at the front in the summer of
1915.

6 July, 1915.

My dear Murray [Professor Sir Gilbert Murray],

I wrote a letter to Miss Blomfield some time ago describing the
absolute ease and comfort of life in France. I now retract. We
have had our first independent tour in the trenches now, and
war in its most Grim, Ghastly and Terrible forms burst upon us.
That, at least, is the impressions I got from reading the men's
letters since they come back into billets. Personally, I did not
find things quite so lurid, but one day I will write you a letter
in the style of the more imaginative of our men, and if that
doesn't make you feel we've been 'bearing the brunt', which
again is their favourite way of describing it, I don't know what
will. However, perhaps you'd like a more sober account to
begin with. My platoon had the doubtful honour of being in the
most dangerous part of the line we were holding, and had
nearly half the battalion casualties, but they were not serious.
Our welcome was a little unnerving. We were in a place where
the lines run at curious angles, and in a sort of corner, where the

45

trenches were about 120 yards apart, the Germans had exploded a mine nearly half way across some months ago. About an hour after we had got in there was a tremendous explosion, the earth flew up, from a place that seemed quite near us, fifty yards or so into the air, and at once the German rifles and machine-guns opened a heavy fire. The men were a good bit scared, and for a moment or two I wondered if the Germans were going to rush. My job seemed to be to steady things a bit, and it would have been a fine occasion for a dramatic speech. The only remarks that came into my mind, however, were 'Sentries look to your periscopes and the rest keep low'. It was prosaic, but the opportunities for romance do not occur to you at the moment—at least, they didn't to me. After all, it is no use saying 'Remember Waterloo' to my men, for most of them have never heard of the battle, and would think that I was referring to the railway station.

My job, however, really began later. There used to be a listening patrol in the old mine-crater near which the new mine had been exploded. I had to go out, as commander of that part of the trench, and find out what really had happened, and what could be done about occupying the place or preventing the Germans from getting it. So I crawled out and reconnoitred. Do you know the policemen's chorus in 'The Pirates of Penzance'—'with cat-like tread upon the foe I steal'? It was absurdly like that, I didn't know where the new mine had blown up nor where the old one was precisely, nor what was the way in nor anything important. So I had to make my way round and look over the rim very anxiously and carefully, with a revolver in my hand, hoping that there would be no Germans waiting to shove a bayonet at me. Lying down between the lines and hearing the bullets whiz over you is really not at all bad fun, and I quite enjoyed one place where I could be completely covered, as I thought, and survey the German trenches about thirty yards off. But my pleasure was rather damped the next morning when I saw from a periscope that the place was right in the line of fire from the English trenches. I thought at the time that the ping-pongs were rather close, but I couldn't quite see where our trenches ran. I don't think there really was much danger about it, except that the lines run across one another in a very odd shape, and it was difficult to be quite sure which way the firing was really going. After my first two nights I settled

46

where to put my patrol, and what work must be done to screen them, and I felt quite secure about it. For by a process, not to be called reasoning, you expect that after you've found a place unoccupied for two nights running you won't find it occupied the third. I had a little trouble the last night, however, for one of the sentries thought he saw two Germans looking into the approach by which we reached the mouth of the craters. He had really just lost his head, but I had to get a party ready in case of attack and make another reconnaissance. Of course there was nothing there, but it meant a certain loss of sleep, and really that is my chief complaint of the trenches. Out of 112 hours I got twelve hours' sleep, and that entirely in the daytime. I am naturally a very sleepy animal, and do not like losing my rest.

The other thing I hate is the artillery. I detest them and all their works. They stay three or four miles behind in the most comfortable billets imaginable and just amuse themselves by loosing off their instruments of torture at the infantry. It is all very well to talk of a clean death in battle, but it's not a clean death that the artillery deals. It means arms and legs torn off and men mangled out of recognition by their great hulking bullies of guns. I would sweep them all away and settle it by the quiet and decent methods of the infantry. Not that we have suffered a heavy bombardment. The whole thing is tit-for-tat. We break their parapet one night—the next morning they break ours. They drop some rifle grenades into our trenches— we set up an infernal machine to do the same to theirs. I had great fun finding out how to work it. Most of these grenades on both sides fail to go off, I fancy. In general, if one side is quiet, the other waits a long time before provoking him. The real depressing thing about this trench warfare is plainly that you know your own casualties, but you have very little idea of theirs. It's not like fighting in the open, where you know at least that you have gained a mile or lost it. It spoils the beauty of these wars of attrition so much not to know which side is being worn away most.

Flies are a great nuisance, and mosquitoes also. The most cheering things I've heard really are that the German sanitary arrangements are much inferior to ours and the health of their troops worse. Our men are certainly very well, very kindly treated by the people here and their friends at home, and getting better food on the whole than at Aldershot, or indeed than in many of their own homes. I am writing to thank Lady Mary [Lady Mary Murray] for her gifts. You really overwhelm me with kindness, and I feel that I ought to be having a much more uncomfortable time to justify it. At least, I don't have the trial of reading all these wretched papers and politicians whining about the war. I was so glad to see your letter about Northcliffe and the Bishop of Pretoria. [Murray had attacked Lord Northcliffe and the Bishop for their 'defeatism'.] Of course, the right thing is not to buy the *Times* [at that time pessimistic about the war] though it's a difficult habit to break, and my mess still takes it. The trouble is that a lot of the complaints seem well grounded, though nothing can excuse the way they are put, nor the uselessness of crying over spilt milk. The poor old Grand Duke, I'm afraid, is really on the way to Nijni Novgorod at last. [A reference to the Russian retreat in the face of overwhelming German attack.] But I expect your faith in the Russian autocracy is unbroken. It's no use my advising you to read pessimistic papers now. What everybody seems to need in the Press now is a good strong dose of Winston Churchill. I wish he were a newspaper editor instead of a Cabinet Minister. I will send you some more news soon, and try to make it less personal history. But I must not divulge secrets about the Army—even if I knew any—whereas if the Germans capture this letter it won't do them any good to know that I have been listening to the noises in their trenches with great disfavour. I told you, didn't I, that I had been with Gillespie [see his letters in this collection]. I wish I were nearer Jack Medley, but I'm not at all sorry that my place is not in the Holy of Holies [i.e. at H.Q.]. To be near him is the only thing that would console me for being shoved away back there.

My love to you all.

One of Heath's brother officers asked him to write a letter modelled on those written home by the men and which the officers censored. The officer planned to send the letter to some friends who had posted him a cake. When he went back on the idea Heath sent the letter to one of his own friends. It is realistic in the crudity of construction and poverty of thought Heath attributes to the ordinary soldier of his time.

August, 1915.

Dear Mrs.

Just a few loving lines in answer to your kind and loving letter and Thanking you for the two beautiful parcels which has come in very handy, the Cake was quiet unbroken and me and my mates enjoyed it very much in the trenches. Dear Mrs. we have been six days and nights under fire, but the Germans will never advance near they are afraid of our rifle fire. I keeps popping off at them all through the night and they keeps their nappers low you can bet. All the boys are well and in the best of spirits. It is a bit OT hear but we are doing our bit and dear Mrs. I am surprised that Tom Grayson has not yet enlisted. I call it a big shame four of us from one family Out here bearing the brunt and him crawling round the pubs and won't even send me a Woodbine. dear Mrs. you know young Ginger Dempster as was my mate he as gone to the salvidge collecting old iron from the German canons they are busted up all round hear something awful. We are back now for a bit of a rest and we can do with it too but every night we dig trenches under fire. We shall go into the trenches again soon and after that we come home on leave so that I shall see you and the two dear Babies again. Ho what joyfull times we shall have when this is all over. We are fed up with it but we keep smiling. Dear Mrs. I will close for the censor will not let us say anything. Hoping you are in the Pink as it leaves me,

From your ever lovin
Brother-in-Law.

' *The prettiest sight I've ever seen* '

Corporal R. J. Jeffares of the Canadian Army wrote the following letter to a friend on the staff of the Canadian Bank of Commerce, Vancouver branch, where he had himself been employed. Jeffares was later reported missing in action.

18 August, 1915.

We are playing cricket, baseball and football and giving concerts every week. I was just thinking last night what a queer thing life was out here. I was lying on the cricket field about seven o'clock, looking towards the town, which is a very old one, and it was a lovely night with a magnificent sunset, the old round tower standing up against the sky was like a scene from the 'Arabian Nights', and for the modern side of life, all around us the Germans were shelling our aeroplanes. Almost overhead there was a duel going on between a British biplane and a German Taube. You could see the sparks of flame from the machine-guns and our fellows must have hit him for he turned and ran for home, and as he was much faster than our machine got clear away from it, but was hit by our anti-aircraft guns and had to descend in our lines. A duel in the air between British, French and German planes is the most exciting and the prettiest sight I've ever seen. As a kind of side-show at the same time that the duel in the air was going on, the Germans were making a hideous row dropping 'Coal boxes', otherwise shells, big ones, in a village half a mile away trying to locate one of our heavy batteries.

6

'A hamper from Harrods weekly' (1915)
'I shall never look on warfare as fine or sporting again' (1917)

Graham Greenwell was eighteen years old in 1914. He had left Winchester that summer and was to have gone to Oxford in October. Instead, he attended the Public Schools Officers' Camp and was there gazetted to the 4th Battalion, Oxfordshire and Buckinghamshire Light Infantry. He went to war a callow second-lieutenant—'I have had a most ripping day' on 24 May, 1915—and survived to be a critical captain—'[it was] all for nothing . . . a heart-breaking business' on 20 April, 1917. He won the Military Cross for gallant leadership. Greenwell's letters to his mother are valuable for they show the rapid maturing of a young man's thoughts and emotions under the forced growth of a war.

24 May, 1915.
*Ploegsteert Wood.**
[Plugstreet, to most soldiers]

I am now at last among all my friends and have seen them all, including dear Hermon: I am supremely happy and have had

* Neither Greenwell nor other British writers were guilty of breaking security by mentioning place-names; they were added later.

the most interesting day of my life. I can't believe it is true. At
11 o'clock our *horses* came round and Alan Gibson [Alan K.
Gibson, Transport Officer] and I mounted in the most divine
sunshine to *ride* up to the trenches! I felt most contented and
told him that I could scarcely believe we were so near the war.
Our horses shied at all the steam trolleys and motor-vans, and
otherwise were good: it was a glorious ride. In a few minutes
we came to the village and then I first saw what war meant. It
was shelled to pieces and almost every house had a hole in it,
although the women and children, poor wretches, were still
there! We were riding along gaily enough when we met dear
old Hugh Deacon who had come in to buy wine. We pulled up
and chatted with him until Gibson laughed and said, 'Well, I
am not going to stand just here much longer'—we were at a
cross-roads, just the place for shells. Ten minutes later, the
Germans put their daily quota of five or six big shells into the
little village, and Deacon told us later that he was just buying
some *vin ordinaire* when a shell burst just outside the shop and
the poor woman bolted for her life downstairs and absolutely
refused to reappear, even to take his money. Of course we heard
the shells going overhead, but the horses didn't mind a bit. We
dismounted just behind the wood in which our regiment is, and
walked through it along specially raised wooden platforms made
by the Engineers which intersect it. They all have names: the
main road through to the trenches is called Regent Street.
Hyde Park Corner, the Strand and Piccadilly are all official
names, so I feel quite at home. I lunched with Hermon and his
Company officers—six of them— in a beautiful wooden cabin:
we had fresh meat, peas and fried potatoes, then tinned fruits
and cheese and coffee. Hermon was very glad to see me again
and everyone is very nice.

Conny took me round this afternoon and I went through all
our trenches with him: they are most weird and quite different
from what one expects, not a long continuous line, but all zig-
zagged anywhere and very bad ones. I looked through all the
periscopes and peepholes, and had a quick look at the German
trenches round a corner; they are only 40 yards away and it was
most interesting and amusing. I kept meeting all my old friends
round different corners. We had tea in a little dug-out with six
other officers in the trenches, cakes galore and jam: very
pleasant. Conny had three or four pot-shots with a rifle through

a peephole. Our Company is having its four days' rest in the reserve trenches, so I was free to go round with him; but there are lots of fatigue parties for the men which make life very unpleasant I believe.

At night the reserve companies—two out of four—man their trenches and sleep in them. We may not take off our clothes or boots at all. Luckily there is a ruined cottage in the middle of our line which is our Company Headquarters and Mess. I have just had an excellent dinner in it, a beautifully cooked beef-steak pudding and rhubarb tart with cream; your present of a ham arrived to our great joy.

I get up at six tomorrow to serve out a *rum* ration to my platoon. . . . This is a very quiet part of the line at present, though the guns go on day and night. The shells start with a heavy dull bang and then come through the air in the most extraordinary way just like a railway train. The anti-aircraft guns are great fun and very pretty to watch: first a deep plomp like a rocket and then a little cloud of white smoke in the air with an aeroplane gaily circling above it, always quite safe.

I have had a most ripping day. I can't remember ever having had so much pleasure and excitement, seeing so many old friends and experiencing such new sensations. I can see that one must be resigned to keeping one's clothes on all day and night for weeks at a time and to getting sleep always in the open and only for an hour or two; but it is all so delightfully fresh after England that the unpleasant side of it does not strike me, though all my friends have been trying to instil into me the gospel of 'frightfulness'.

I have been made Mess President by Conny and he says that as long as things are packed *very securely* all is well. Good cheeses of the small Dutch variety and chocolates are welcome but Harrods will make suggestions. In Hermon's Company they have a hamper from Harrods weekly—but I need not tell you what I want because you always know best and anticipate me.

We have great fun inviting people to lunch and other meals and are quite a gay party.

13 June, 1915.
Trenches, St. Ives,
Douve Valley.

Best thanks for the ham and the tongue. The beautiful large

cake has just appeared on our luncheon table at which I am writing, *clean* and cool and with only the distant crash of a gun and the very occasional ping of a bullet against the parapet to disturb me. On our table there is some nice nobbly lettuce in a bowl with some very loud onions, some cold beef, a bottle of white *vin ordinaire* and another of table water; a Dutch cheese, some small cheese biscuits, some tinned fruit in a bowl, jam and marmalade, and lastly your cake. On the sideboard there are numerous varieties of potted meats, cigarettes, chocolates, pickles, dates, acid drops, revolvers, field-glasses, the *Bystander*, *Punch* and *Times*, so we might quite well be in rooms at Oxford, mightn't we?

> *27 August, 1915.*
> *Hébuterne.*

I am so hot that I can scarcely control my pencil.

I have just been having a tremendous fight against Conny and Freddie Grisewood, armed with long sticks and apples. It is much more fun than real war.

The weather is glorious; I was out again last night under a full moon, putting up barbed wire defences; but there was such a glorious moon that I quite enjoyed it.

> *17 August, 1916.*
> *Skyline Trench, Ovillers,*
> *Somme.*

You wouldn't be able to conceive the filthy and miserable surroundings in which I am writing this note—not even if you were accustomed to the filthiest slums in Europe.

I am sitting in the bottom of an old German dug-out about ten or twelve feet under the earth with three other officers and about ten men, orderlies and runners; the table is littered with food, equipment, candle grease and odds and ends. The floor is covered with German clothing and filth. The remains of the trench outside is blown to pieces, and full of corpses from the different regiments which have been here lately, German and English. The ground is ploughed up by enormous shell-holes; there isn't a single landmark to be seen for miles except a few gaunt sticks where trees once were. The stench is well-nigh intolerable, but thank God I have just found the remains of a tube of frozacalone which I have rubbed under my nose. Everyone is absolutely worn out with fatigue and hunger.

Yesterday while trying to find the regiment we were relieving, I was very slightly wounded by a piece of shrapnel to the left of my left eye. It knocked me over and stunned me a bit, but was only a flesh wound and is healed now except for a bruise.

I wandered on round these awful remains of trenches with my bugler, simply sickened by the sights and smells, until I found some poor devils cowering in the filth, where they had been for forty-eight hours. I moved them back. Soon after this I felt rather dizzy and went back to Battalion headquarters where the Colonel was very kind and made me lie down on a German bed for a rest. Later in the afternoon I went down to the doctor, who has a fine dressing station in a huge German dug-out. There I rested and spent the night and came back here this morning.

Thank Heaven we are due to be relieved in an hour or two, when we shall go back to some trenches behind, though they will, of course, be only comparatively better. Tomorrow morning I hope the whole regiment will be relieved and go back.

I shall never look on warfare either as fine or sporting again. It reduces men to shivering beasts: there isn't a man who can stand shell-fire of the modern kind without getting the blues. The Anzacs are fine fellows, but they say Gallipoli was a garden party to this show.

20 April, 1917.
Outpost Line Guillemont Farm.

We were relieved last night about midnight after an exciting little dust-up and I didn't get my men back to their billets till 4.30 this morning. We were all dead tired although, thank Heaven, I had my horse on the journey back. I slept till about midday today and then had 'brunch' in bed.

Last night we got orders to do a little attack before being relieved against a small strong-point which lay between us and the great Hindenburg Line. Unfortunately this had already been attempted three or four days before and been a ghastly failure and the Bosche was very much on the 'qui vive', keeping up a constant stream of Verey lights in front of it. My Company was holding the outpost line to the right and so were not concerned save with the possibly unpleasant effects of hostile shelling.

I thought it better to withdraw my headquarters and reserve

men to a deep sunken road some way behind and I sat down about 7.30 at the end of a telephone prepared to listen to other people's bravery. Our artillery started bombarding the strongpoint at 7.30, but with only about twenty-five guns in all—just enough to give the show away.

As it was still light the Germans could see our fellows (D Company) going over and appear practically to have wiped out the first wave of the attack—killing one Platoon Commander, an amusing Scotty called Dinwoodie, wounding the other, and knocking out most of the N.C.O.'s. The Company Commander then took over the other two platoons but also got held up. Finally, I heard him telephoning back to Battalion headquarters to say that he was lying out with the remnants of his Company about two hundred yards in front of the German position, and that he wanted some more men and some more gunfire in front of him. It was rather extraordinary to be able to listen to the whole thing at the end of a wire and to hear the poor devil who was getting men killed all round him and was expecting to be crumped any moment talking to his C.O., who was giving him instructions and then himself getting on to the Brigade.

I shall take jolly good care to cut myself completely off from anyone behind next time I do a show. They telephoned back first, if you please, to the Brigade and then to the Divisional General (who was out) for leave to send over another company to help the first. The G.S.O.1. [General Staff Officer 1] said that he couldn't advise without the General's leave. Consequently the Company was ordered to come back and we all went home to bed, with a Company weaker by 45 men wounded, nine killed, four missing, two officers gone and all for nothing. Thank Heaven it wasn't my Company: it would have been a heart-breaking business. Personally I *will* not take instructions from the men behind once the show has been launched. It is fatal and has been proved to be so hundreds of times. The man on the spot must be given power to decide. Tonight I believe the people who relieved us are attacking with three battalions! The Staff lives, but God knows if it ever learns much. Fortunately they get the right men now in command, which makes a lot of difference and they are constantly sending people home. But it's among the lower grades that we lack the qualities so much in evidence on the German side.

Criticism of incompetent staff work was common among fighting officers. The action Greenwell describes was one of the last in the battle of Arras, launched by the British as a preliminary to the Nivelle Offensive (Second Battle of the Aisne). Arras was a tactical British victory but there was no breakthrough and the British suffered 84,000 casualties to the German 70,000. Greenwell was right when he implied that results could have been better and casualties fewer had the men on the spot had greater authority. The Nivelle Offensive also failed, the French suffering 120,000 casualties.

Greenwell finished the war on the Italian front. His last war letter was written from Italy on 26 December, 1918. With the war over six weeks, his own survival assured and memories of slaughter already blunted, he could write to his mother '. . . It will be very hard to leave the regiment after so many years. . . . Could you ever have guessed how much I should enjoy the war?'

He was demobilized in January 1919 and went to Oxford to read History. He joined the Stock Exchange in 1923 and served during World War II in the Oxfordshire & Buckinghamshire Light Infantry. He was still living in 1972.

7
'The attack was glorious'

Early in October 1915 a young Canadian and a young German both wrote home to describe their reactions to being involved in battle. Their letters—the Canadian's matter-of-fact, the German's impassioned—make an interesting contrast. The Canadian, Lieutenant J. S. Williams, a bank clerk, was in the front line at Spanbrok-Molen below the Messines Ridge in front of Kemmel, Belgium, He survived the war.

3 October, 1915.

Well, I've been through it and out of it again. That is to say, I have just had five days and five nights in the front line trenches, and am back a little way for a five days' rest. It was pretty much what I imagined it to be. The first hour to me was uncanny, because it seems so incredible to think that only fifty yards off were men aching to get a glimpse of my devoted head to put a bullet through it. After that, I only felt indifference. It really is most extraordinary what one can get accustomed to. Whizz-bangs [shells] and bullets were flying about at the time, and when you found that they missed *you*, you began to feel, at any rate I did, that they would never hit you. But the real 'corkers' are those 'Jack Johnsons', or 'Coal Boxes' [heavy shells]. You hear the brute coming a long way off with the noise of an express train. It's no good hiding anywhere, because you would only be buried by the debris, so you sit tight, hold your breath and pray to God it won't hit you. Then when it lands a most appalling explosion takes place, shakes the earth all round, and then . . . you breathe once more. It certainly is a delightfully indescribable feeling, waiting and wondering where they are going to drop.

My dugout in the trench had other occupants, things with lots of legs, also swarms of rats and mice, so I didn't feel at all lonely. I think I have slept in every conceivable place of filth there is now, and the most extraordinary thing is that you do sleep. I did not have my clothes off my back for the whole time I was in the trenches, and it rained the whole time. We were all wet through. The excitement counteracted the chill. I had a most delightful bath this morning in a . . . convent! The Nuns filled the bath with hot water and just when I was beginning to get anxious, they gracefully retired. I do not think any of my friends would have recognized the walking pillar of mud, that disentangled itself from muddy surrounds and wended its weary way to the rest camp here, as the once immaculate bank clerk!!!

It is perfectly true that the German and English converse from their various trenches; the remarks are not fit for drawing-room publication, but they are very humorous.

The people who live all round here are about 1,000 years behind the times, and even then do not use the smallest grain of horse sense in laying out their little villages, or even farm houses. They have their refuse pits bang up against the pump, and all that sort of thing.

The German Alfred Vaeth, born 25 December, 1889, at Krozingen, Baden, had been a student of philosophy at Heidelberg before becoming sergeant in an infantry regiment. He was killed in action, near Leintrey, France, only four days after writing this letter.

12 October, 1915.

The attack was terribly beautiful! the most beautiful and at the same time the most terrible thing I have ever experienced. Our artillery shot magnificently, and after two hours (the French take seventy) the position was sufficiently prepared for German Infantry. The storm came, as only German Infantry can storm! It was magnificent the way our men, especially the youngest, advanced, magnificent! Officers belonging to other regiments, who were looking on, have since admitted they had never seen anything like it! In the face of appalling machine-gun fire they went on with a confidence which nobody could ever attempt to equal. And so the hill, which had been stormed in vain three times, was taken in an hour. The booty was greater than was stated in the Order of the Day.

But now comes the worst part—to hold the hill! Bad, very bad days are in front of us. One can scarcely hope to get through safe and sound. The French guns are shooting appallingly, and every night there are counter-attacks and bombing raids. Where I am we are only about 20 yards apart. Now, when one has again got through the easiest part of the attack, one shudders at the thought that one may be torn to bits by a shell in a trench, covered with dirt, and so end—in the mud and filth! We should all like so much to live a few months longer until an advance towards final victory has been made here.

The attack was glorious!

' *The drivel of those who write despatches* '

Six weeks later another German soldier, Johannes Haas, born 12 March, 1892, at Erfde, Schleswig, saw nothing glorious in his field of combat in Champagne. Haas, a student of theology in Leipzig before the war, was killed on 1 June, 1916, at Verdun.

27 November, 1915.

To his parents.

. . . In what way have we sinned, that we should be treated worse than animals? Hunted from place to place, cold, filthy and in rags, we wander about like gipsies, and in the end are destroyed like vermin! Will they *never* make peace!

At this time many German soldiers felt they were not being adequately supported by the people at home and were bitterly critical of German politicians for what they regarded as their lack of understanding of the soldiers' plight. The same complaints frequently occur in the letters of Allied soldiers; in this, as in so many other things, the frontline soldiers of both sides had much in common. In a letter of 29 January, 1916, Johannes Haas was explicit about his complaints.

A man called Reinhold in my section had a letter from his wife saying that she had pawned all the furniture except the indispensable beds. And then the Lieutenants wonder that the men don't want to go on fighting. The 'Champagne and Wine Johnnies' [the German profiteers and warmongers] are enjoying themselves while *we* are dying in filth, and celebrating Christmas with a spoonful and a half of jam and fourteen pieces of sugar.

The only man who has any sympathy for or confidence in the Private Soldier is that ranter Liebknecht. 'Scheidemann and Legien should join the Agrarian Party; they will never again be returned to the Reichstag as Social Democrats.' That, and not the drivel of those who write despatches, represents what the Field Greys [the German soldiers' own term for themselves] really feel. I don't agree with the popular saying 'that there will only be peace when the bullets are aimed in the opposite direction', but, all the same, there will be a fearful awakening some day! It will be well then for those who can pass away into eternity still believing in the Fatherland, for that time will be worse than the war.

'Never any expressions of hatred'

Hugo Müller was one of many German soldiers to express surprise at finding enemy soldiers devoid of hatred for the Germans and confident of the justness of their own cause. Born on 5 May, 1892, at Buchholz, Müller was a law student in Leipzig. He was killed on 18 October, 1916, near Warlencourt, in the Ancre Valley.

> *At Agny, near Arras,*
> *17 October, 1915.*

To his family.

I am enclosing a French field-postcard, which I want you to put with my war-souvenirs. It came out of the letter-case of a dead French soldier. It has been extremely interesting to study the contents of the letter-cases of French killed and prisoners. The question frequently recurs, just as it does with us: 'When will it all end?'

To my astonishment I practically never found any expression

of hatred or abuse of Germany or German soldiers. On the other hand, many letters from relations revealed an absolute conviction of the justice of their cause, and sometimes also of confidence in victory. In every letter mother, fiancée, children, friends, whose photographs were often enclosed, spoke of a joyful return and a speedy meeting—and now they are all lying dead and hardly even buried between the trenches, while over them bullets and shells sing their gruesome dirge.

'The present is the thing'

Stephen Hewett was born in India in 1893 and educated at the Benedictine college of Downside between 1905 and 1911. He had just completed his third year at Balliol, Oxford—where he read History—when war broke out. Commissioned into the Warwickshire Regiment, Second-Lieutenant Hewett disappeared while leading his platoon in an attack during the battle of the Somme, 22 July, 1916. His company commander, Captain Bryson, wrote, 'He was a fine officer in every way, loved and respected by his men . . . He never flinched for a moment and worthily upheld the traditions of the regiment and, of course, of Oxford men. . . .'

16 May, 1916, France.

To a friend, Hubert Secretan.

I wonder when it will be my turn for leave; I have already been out here three months and more, but do not expect to get away for as many months again. From May 1 to 6 I had the good luck to be behind the line, having a very jolly rest in a little village, and being instructed in a species of trench howitzer, for which I am now supposed to be qualified as a reserve officer for the Brigade. This is a great nuisance, for I am very keen on my Battalion, and especially on my company and platoon, but most especially on my Coy. Commander—the Oriel [College] man. He is only twenty-one years old, but most efficient: the idol of officers and men. Bryson is his name . . . I wish we had all known him in the good days, and I hope we may all know him in good days to come. Really there are some awfully good officers here, one of them an old school-friend of mine: the men too are of a distinctly good class, keen, intelligent, and to my mind remarkably good soldiers. How well-bred non-banausic [sic] men can be as brave as they are, and how they can stick what they have to stick (where even officers have a fairly rough time), passes my comprehension. I am very keen altogether on the men, though there is not much that one can do for them, and though their work is largely of a kind in which officers can hardly collaborate: still, I had a most enjoyable time a week ago with four of them, wiring in the No Man's Land, for over an hour and a half.

You do not mind if I just go on chatting to you in this letter, without forethought or sequence: perhaps that is really the best way of conveying the true 'atmosphere'—besides, I feel in a chatty mood, being at ease in support billets, with a cigar in my mouth and in my ears the loud but soothing noise of a heavy strafe which does not immediately affect us:

Suave . . . magnum alterius spectare laborem [It's pleasant to watch someone else having a hard time.] There, that shows what heartless beasts we quickly become out here.

In a very short time I shall be going up to finish my third period in the trenches. In between the periods, and ushered in by a long exhilarating night-march, with cannonades and rockets away on our flank, we enjoy a bit of rest in reserve billets behind the line (Locus refrigerii, lucis et pacis) [A place of refreshment, light and peace], a place of lighter duties, longer sleep, pyjamas and beds, bridge, football, and all the things which appeal to our now wholly unspiritual tempers. At Oxford we were taught to laugh at a certain 'fiction' called The Natural Man: out here he is a gross and palpable reality— material, inchoate, incoherent, disconnected, IL-LOGICAL, but a better man for all that, and a stronger, than ever he was in Blighty. 'Warm work! . . . but, mark you, I would not be elsewhere for worlds.' I loathe it healthily and heartily, but I am sure it is doing me good.

We happen to be in a not too terrifically lively spot, but of course no place in the line is a health-resort. Curiously enough my most alarming and dangerous experience was on my first morning here and my first entry into 'the beaten zone', and my two most unpleasant ones both took place during my first week in trenches. One gets hardened in some degree to the terrors and labours, but on the other hand one loses the sense of freshness and excitement and is tormented by the demon of boredom.

As for the duration of the war, you know much more about the probabilities than I do, but I should like to know what you would feel about it all if you were here. Verbum non amplius!

Poor old Master! [A reference to the death of the Master of Balliol] I feel a strange sense as of a personal loss even now,— a shadow over the sunlight in that beloved quadrangle. The other day I saw among the killed 2nd Lt. Vincent Hobson—an Oriel man who used to attend the Master's lectures on Appian, and I remembered the intonation with which the old man used to pronounce that name in his Roll-call. Ah, me, the voice is silent, the dust is settling on 'The Civil War', and the Pulpit and the desks are empty.

Poor old Hubert! It is poor enough fun out here, but it must be a great deal worse for you—fettered to an office-stool and held back in the leash.

Hewett several times expressed his surprise at finding that the common soldier was not only human but could be intelligent and perceptive. On 19 June, 1916, having just censored some letters, Hewett wrote to his mother: 'What a lesson it is to read the thoughts of men, often as refined and sensitive as we have been made by the advantages of birth and education, yet living under conditions much harder and more disgusting than my own!' In one of his last letters, to F. F. Urquhart, his tutor at Balliol, he became eloquent about the joys of Switzerland.

13 July, 1916.

... My heaven, Slig! somebody has just brought in a magazine illustrated with many photographs of Switzerland, and for a whole evening I have recaptured

'The first virgin passion of a soul
Communing with the glorious universe.'

That is all past.

'Toutes ces choses sont passées, comme l'ombre et comme le vent.' But one thinks of them now—'comme un dernier rayon, comme un dernier Zephyr raniment la fin d'un beau jour.' [All these things have passed away like shadows and wind, just as a last ray (of sunshine) and a final breeze revitalize the end of a beautiful day.]

64

We are 'for it' now at last. Yes, I do think we shall soon be earning either a big head-line or a place in the casualty-list. We may be leaving any moment (we are still in the Corot village) marching or entraining anywhither. But we shall not pass the familiar stations of La Roche, Cluses, Bonneville, Sallanches! Ah, the thought of the Prarion is too impossible for realization: it would make one burst this human frame with dizzy rapture. But the present is the thing, the great present. We ask nothing better. . . .

'And yet, one is merry there'

If young soldiers could see war as 'ripping' (Greenwell) or view an attack as 'glorious' (Vaeth), older men had a more dispassionate attitude. One of them was Ernest Boughton Nottingham, a stockbroker's clerk, who, at thirty-eight, enlisted in 1915 in the 15th London Regiment. He quickly became a non-commissioned officer and won the British Distinguished Conduct Medal and the French Croix de Guerre.

To a friend, Charles Williams.   *France, 27/3/16.*

My dear Charles,

. . . I will tell you a story. In the long ward, a cheerful contented undertone of conversation. Two fires burning and the occupants lying comfortably on mattresses or stretchers. Fed, warm, cosy. Far from shells, bullets, bombs, minnies [slang for a type of shell], gas.—There's the rain again. It beats furiously on the skin window-panes and on the low roof. Up there, in uncompleted lines—the enemy seized first and second some month or more ago, not from us—the boys stand in mud and water thro' the night—there has been much snow and the rain completes its evaporation into water. Silent the sentries on the fire steps, peering across 'no man's-land'. The reliefs not yet on duty stand or crouch in their appointed bays. A peg of wood will help suspend a ground sheet against the dripping clay wall and a man may flatten himself under this looking like part of the trench. Rain, pitiless rain, soaking and numbing.—And so to wear the night away.—Blessed the tot of rum, which unlocks quickly a man's reserves and allows him to 'carry on', for the necessary hours. But a man is not in advanced lines all the time, and in rotation, he comes back to 'support' lines where are 'dug-outs', sometimes good, sometimes mere crowded holes in the wet clay. Anyhow the night passes, even the worst ones, and the morning nip of rum energizes for breakfast making. Happy the section with a little kindling wood.

Breakfast—magic rite, it makes the world a paradise again!! Since I became transport corporal I've missed some discomfort, but I know all about it. Once again, marvel at the reserves which every man carries which make endurance passably easy once one is 'up against it'. But here, in the warm with my three blankets I lie and listen to the rain, and see the trenches knee-deep in parts. I feel uncomfortable—and yet enjoy the extreme luxury.

I hope you'll be satisfied if I write as I can—about things in my mind, and you write your letters just as you do. I need not tell you how I enjoy the play of your nimble mind, even tho' my experiences here and my reading of events, seem to have hardened me against many tendencies you [exhibit]. Some day, God willing, we'll talk about things again.—As you say, I know there's another world than this hard, cheerful objective life we lead—I feel it momentarily (and feel sad) at the sound of a train, or a church bell, or the scent and sight of a flower, or the green of a hedge. But not now in the ecstasy of a lark.—That is inseparably connected with 'stand to' in trenches.—So often from Festubert onwards have I heard him singing joyously in the early dawn. I spoke of the hardening of experience. Here's an instance. All the innumerable stories of stay-at-home writers about the genius of place—I've just come from where fifty thousand bodies lie, bones and barbed wire everywhere, skeletons bleached if one takes a walk over the frightfully con-tested and blown up hill.—Boots and bones protruding from one's dug-out walls, and yet—one is merry there.—At the mid-night hour one sees, nor expects to see, nothing of wraiths, or of the spirits of countless brave ones who met there a violent death!—

Yours,
Ernest.

Becoming a sergeant, Nottingham met his own violent end; he died of wounds on 7 June, 1917, at the age of forty.

' *The entire conversion of our whole attitude* '

Another older soldier was Robert Furley Callaway, who had been a mission priest in Africa before returning to England to join the army as a chaplain. Dissatisfied with this role, Callaway sought a commission as a combatant officer and joined the Sherwood Foresters. He, too, perished on the Somme, 13 September, 1916, at the age of forty-four.

2/9/16.

To his Wife.

. . . Before the route march yesterday the whole Brigade formed up in a cornfield to listen to a lecture by a Scotch Major. It was extraordinarily good, but to me the interest of the lecture lay not so much in the lecture itself as in what the lecture stood for —the entire conversion of our whole attitude of mind as a nation. For it was instruction as to how best to *kill* (with the bayonet), and every possible device that had been found by experience useful to enable a man to kill as many Germans as possible, was taught. As one writes it down it sounds the most hideous brutality, and yet yesterday I don't suppose there was an officer or man present who did not agree that if the war is to be won we must fight to kill. Personally I still shudder at the idea of sticking six inches of cold steel into another man's body or having his steel stuck into my body, but I shudder merely with the natural instinct of repulsion which is common to at least all educated people. I don't shudder because I think it any more wrong of me as a priest. I have never for a single moment regretted becoming a combatant. In one way I can say with St. Paul, 'I glory in the things which concern my own infirmities.' I am proud of just those very things which other people think must be such a bore for me, e.g., coming down in rank [as a chaplain he had been a captain], being under the orders of boys of eighteen, having to trudge along on foot, etc. and for that reason I rejoiced even when I gave up the Lewis Gun job, though everybody thought me a fool to do so.

Few men would willingly surrender their control of the Lewis machine-gun; its rapid rate of fire was better insurance than the slower rate of a rifle.

8

'Men at war become more bestial'

Yet another victim of the Somme slaughter was Second-Lieutenant William Henry Ratcliffe of the South Staffordshire Regiment. A student of chemistry before enlistment, he was killed in action on 1 July, at the age of nineteen. In the first paragraph of his last letter to his parents, Ratcliffe framed a bitter antithesis.

June, 1916.

. . . Another Sunday has arrived, and so far is not any more like a Sunday than the last. According to orders there was a church parade this morning but it was cancelled, but may come off later in the day, and so I have been throwing bombs this morning.

If the people in England who try to abolish the day of rest could come out here they would feel the need of it. Apart from the time afforded for spiritual recreation, a day of rest would be something to look forward to, and would break the monotony of life, and the monotony and dull routine is the chief objection to this life. Of course everyone understands the impossibility of giving the A.S.C. [Army Service Corps] and the men actually in the trenches a day's rest; but why a battalion which is out of the trenches for a rest can't stop forming fours and sloping arms for one day I don't know.

I was reading a story in one of the magazines that you sent out which was trying to prove that this war had a good effect on men's minds and made them more religious than they were before. Whilst I was in Jersey I really thought that this was the case, and I believe I wrote and told you so, and mentioned what Ian Hamilton [General Sir Ian Hamilton] wrote about the matter. But now that I am out here, I must confess that I almost altogether disagree with Ian Hamilton, and think that war has an almost degrading effect on the minds of soldiers.

What is there out here to raise a man's mind out of the rut? Everywhere one sees preparations for murder; nearly every person one sees is a filthy, dirty man with some implement of destruction about his person. The countryside and the beauties of nature, which, as you know, always have a beneficial effect on a man, are all spoilt by the dust and mud of motor lorries and by huge camps.

Everywhere the work of God is spoiled by the hand of man. One looks at a sunset and for a moment thinks that at least is unsophisticated, but an aeroplane flies across, and puff! puff! and the whole scene is spoilt by clouds of shrapnel smoke!

So you can understand that men who are at war really become more bestial than when at peace, despite popular opinion to the contrary. . . .

' *The effect of war is purifying* '

A German infantryman, Hero Hellwich, writing to his parents, might almost have been expressing a rebuttal of Lieutenant Ratcliffe's views. Born on 15 March, 1896, at Bischofstein, East Prussia, Hellwich had been studying political economy before enlistment. His undated letter (after 6 November, 1916) is prefaced by the note 'I am lying on my tummy by candle-light, although it's daytime. This place lets in the cold and wind and rain all right, but not the daylight.' He was killed on 20 December, 1916, on the Somme.

. . . It is not true that war hardens people's hearts. Anybody who comes back hardened, must have been hard to start with. The effect of war is much more that of purifying and deepening. One thanks God for every day that one is allowed to go on living. If through God's boundless mercy I should be permitted to survive the war, then I will endeavour—however poorly and inadequately I succeed—to prove myself worthy of that mercy.

In war no one is master of his fate. Man's intelligence fails him. He can only say: 'Thy will be done'. I try to be always in such dispositions that, if a bullet or a shell should strike me, I may not die with vain thoughts in my mind. Remember me as I was when at my best.

'*I am desperately anxious to live*'

A soldier who understood the true nature of war was Thomas Michael Kettle, who had a remarkably distinguished civil life before enlistment. Educated at University College, Dublin, he was a barrister, a member of parliament and professor of National Economics at the National University, Dublin, before the age of thirty. He became a captain in the Royal Dublin Fusiliers and was killed in action on 9 September, 1916, aged thirty-two. His last letter—to his brother—was written the day before his death.

8 September, 1916.

... If I live I mean to spend the rest of my life working for perpetual peace. I have seen war and faced modern artillery, and know what an outrage it is against simple men. ...

We are moving up tonight into the battle of the Somme. The bombardment, destruction and bloodshed are beyond all imagination, nor did I ever think the valour of simple men could be quite as beautiful as that of my Dublin Fusiliers. I have had two chances of leaving them—one on sick leave and one to take a staff job. I have chosen to stay with my comrades.

I am calm and happy but desperately anxious to live. ... The big guns are coughing and smacking their shells, which sound for all the world like over-head express trains, at anything from 10 to 1000 per minute on this sector; the men are grubbing and an odd one is writing home. Somewhere the Choosers of the Slain are touching, as in our Norse story they used to touch, with invisible wands those who are to die. ...

'*We should try to build a new Ireland*'

It was indeed a tragedy that Thomas Kettle was among the slain; he would have given Ireland the leadership she so badly needed. Another perceptive and rational Irishman lost in the war was the beloved Willie Redmond—Major William Hoey

Kearney Redmond of the Royal Irish Regiment. Redmond really had no right to be fighting; he was fifty-six years of age, much too old for regimental duty. Nationalist M.P. for East Clare, Redmond had joined the Army at the outbreak of war and was killed in action in France, 7 June, 1917.

The letter he wrote to Sir Arthur Conan Doyle in the spring of 1917 has great significance in view of the troubles which were to beset Ireland half a century later.

... There are a great many Irishmen today who feel that out of this war we should try to build up a new Ireland. The trouble is men are so timid about meeting each other half-way. It would be a fine memorial to the men who have died so splendidly if we could, over their graves, build up a bridge between North and South.

I have been thinking a lot about this lately in France—no one could help doing so when one finds that the two sections from Ireland are actually side by side holding the trenches! No words could do justice to the splendid action of the new Irish soldiers. They never have flinched, they never give any trouble, and they are steady and sober.

Had poor Kettle lived he would have given the world a wonderful account of things out here. I saw a good deal of Kettle, and we had many talks of the unity we both hoped would come out of the war. I have been an extreme Nationalist all my life, and if others as extreme, perhaps, on the other side will only come half-way, then I believe, impossible as it may seem, we should be able to hit upon a plan to satisfy the Irish sentiment and the Imperial sentiment at one and the same time. . . .

' *The present generation is . . . a blood-sacrifice* '

German soldiers writing home from the Somme in the latter half of 1916 were no less sensitive than their British enemy but usually wrote more concisely. All seemed conscious of the enormity of the task they faced. Heinrich Müller, born at Ebersbach in 1893, and formerly a theological student in Heidelberg, spoke for many comrades when he wrote to a younger student.

6 August, 1916.

Now you have got through your *Sekunda* [the 5th Form exam, which secured, among other privileges, that of only one year of military service], and I hope that you will continue to be equally successful in your studies so that you may be a source of satisfaction to your parents and may develop into a capable, well-educated citizen.

Germany's future depends on you boys. The present generation is doomed to be offered up as a blood-sacrifice upon the battle-field. It will be your task some day to restore, in a time of peaceful culture, everything of intellectual and moral value which the war has trampled underfoot.

You see, one after another of our men here goes off to the Great Army. We are all prepared to do that, and we are looking calmly into the cold eye of death. It is simply extraordinary where the strength comes from, which enables us to go on so tenaciously withstanding an enemy who vastly outnumbers us.

Müller was wounded in action and died in a field hospital near Bapaume on 2 October, 1916.

'*The German spirit is invincible*'

His ability to 'go on so tenaciously' until death was probably the result of excellent battalion, company and platoon leadership and the faith nearly all German soldiers had in the strength of the 'German spirit'. Many of them refer to this spirit, which they obviously saw as created by God Himself. A notable young leader inspired by faith was Lieutenant Hans Stegemann, son of a Lutheran pastor and born 28 March, 1893, at Wutzenow. Educated at the High School, Eberswalde, Stegemann was a forestry student before enlistment and was in action from the first days of the war. He was in the breakthrough which nearly reached Paris in August 1914 and was later sent to the Russian front. In the battle of Schwinjuchy, 31 August, 1916, his company of the 165th Regiment lost three officers and fifty men in hand-to-hand fighting. On 6 September, 1916, he wrote to his parents:

Still hale and hearty! Today Excellenz Litzmann [General
Litzmann, commander of 40 Army-Group] decorated me with
the Iron Cross of the First Class. He asked me to remember him
to you, with his kind regards and thanks. His exact words were:
'Greet your parents, especially your mother, from me, and write
this: "I congratulate you on the success of your son, who,
through his smartness and courage, with the assistance of his
splendid Company, has by counter-attacks driven back the
Russians, and by storming Hill 259 averted a grave menace to
my army-group."' [Stegemann held the hill for six hours until
his ammunition was exhausted; then, with the survivors, he
fought his way through the surrounding Russians.]

You may imagine how delighted I am at having earned this
high distinction. I have been recommended for it three times.
My men are almost more delighted than I am. I fully realize
how much I owe to my Company, and not least to those who
are now lying beneath the sod, still and silent, with clenched
teeth, their faces peaceful and almost joyous because in the very
moment of death they knew that victory was ours.

One thing I learnt in those terrible days; even if we are killed
death does not triumph over us, for the German soul will con-
quer, the German spirit is invincible throughout all eternity!
May God preserve our Fatherland!

Lieutenant Stegemann was killed in action on 20 September—
'a perfect example of gallantry in defence of the honour of my
troops', as General Litzmann wrote to Stegemann's parents.
'You may say to yourselves that you have offered up a sacrifice
to the Fatherland, the influence of which will be of lasting
value to the brave 165th Regiment. Our heroes do not die in
vain.'

'*Nothing to complain about*'

Army nursing sisters saw even more of the 'blood-sacrifice'—
Heinrich Müller's phrase—than did the soldiers, but few of
them appear to have written letters about their experiences. A
notable exception was Sister K. E. Luard, who served in France
for almost the entire war, and was awarded the Royal Red
Cross. Her letters are vivid and infinitely human. The three

published here show something of the suffering of the ordinary soldier during the fighting of 1916.

Monday 22 May, 1916, and a Black Day. This German intense bombardment and occupation of our front trenches here at Vimy Ridge, and our desperate attempts to get them back have filled all the C.C.S. [Casualty Clearing Station] and all the worst cases have been scurried up to us as the nearest C.C.S. and the Special Hospital for Abdominals and Chests (which we are now). Just finished in the theatre at midnight—six have died and more will die, and they are still bringing them in— English and French.

They are all being angels of patience and silence, only asking for things, even drinks, when they're absolutely obliged. One who died today said yesterday he had 'nothing to complain about', and he was afraid he was a great trouble! We've had three officers in—one nearly died when he was having his foot taken off. One who had his arm blown off was laid in a dugout and that was blown in on him and it took two hours to dig him out—he was the most cheery of all. Another one was buried for 15 hours—he died this evening. A boy who was trephined [a skull operation] on Saturday night here, and has one eye destroyed and the other covered up, never speaks, but kicks every stitch of clothing off and breaks out into 'Lead, Kindly Light' and 'God Save the King'. Tonight, when a Frenchman in the next bed was raving, he trilled out, 'Thy Kingdom Come, O Lord' in a very sweet voice.

Tuesday night, 23 May. The boy is now singing his hymns in Heaven. Captain R was called up directly we dispersed at midnight last night and was operating all night and doing his dressings this morning till 1. Operating continuously day and night takes a lot out of you—and he had to be ordered off duty for 12 hours after that. Two men died in the night and two more today, besides an officer who died just after he was taken out of the ambulance.

The big ward with beds all round and two lines down the middle is a very sad place—quite full of wrecks—and not one of them ever well enough even to speak to any other one. The next acute hut with beds also is very busy with compound fractures, heads and amputations, and some chests; but the worst chests, and the abdominals and the bombed people with several

74

serious wounds, are in the big ward. Then there's an overflow hut with stretchers, and I have to plant my foot firmly down to prevent the Medical Officers sending heads and amputations there instead of to the bed wards.

We are rather short of men in the detachment, and when eight have to be taken off to dig graves it doesn't add to the simplicity of the work. I've had a night staff put on to the theatre so that the day ones shall not break themselves by doing day and night, but everyone is needed, so it is difficult not to despoil one place in propping up another. . . . I don't know how long the Orderlies and Sisters will last out. The Colonel says he thinks we shall always have this rush because we are so near the Line, but of course since Sunday's attack it has been much worse than usual, and violent and desperate fighting is still going on. I'll be able to tell you more about it later on when it is history: but a whole line of our front trench has been buried with men in it, under thousands and thousands of shells bursting at once dead on to it—and the after events have been neither pretty nor cheering. We are doing a lot of heavy howitzer work tonight very close, which is very distracting.

Last night we were woken up by a great shelling of Hersin again, from about 2 a.m. It was very jumpy. This is going to be a busy night.

We went a few minutes up the road to Hersin after dinner at 9.30 tonight to get a breather, and to see the flashes and hear the lions roaring. It's an incredibly murderous noise.

The 'history' to which Sister Luard referred was violent actions around Vimy Ridge, near Arras, which began on 15 May, when the British exploded mines and captured trenches, and ended on 21 May, when the Germans took British trenches.

Monday, 18 September, 1916. We are all grappling with work all day now; some of it is wonderful, but much of it is nothing but black. There is a boy dying who has his Will in his Pay-book made out 'to my beloved mother'. He looks about 17; he said when I asked him what he'd like me to say to her, 'Tell her, I'm all right; I don't know what to say; I don't want her to be worried, and give her my love!' My three resuscitated gas-gangrene heroes would all have been going down on the train tomorrow, packed to the eyes in splints and rings and slings and pillows, but a cerebro-spinal meningitis was put into my ward and now the whole ward is in quarantine for a week (except me for some illogical reason) and they may not go.

There is a mad boy who is very funny; when you feed him he says, '1, 2, 3 a cup of tea, bread and butter 4, 5, 6, it's 238 now, and 915.' All his thoughts are in numbers. Another boy beckons me to talk to him as I go by, and after the conversation I heard him say, 'Kind owld sowl, ain't she?' The blind boy with both legs off is dying; he doesn't know his legs are off, and is cheerfully delirious most of the time. He calls us 'Teacher' and says, 'Look sharp, dear, go and get it now!' He was murmuring 'Such is life' just now.

'Hush up the worst side of the war'

Had Sister Luard published her letters at the time they might have shocked the British public, large sections of which still considered the war a great adventure in which all right-thinking young men should be involved for the good of God, their King, their country and themselves. Many a mother was pleased to think that her son was doing his bit in the trenches. Occasionally, a soldier wrote a letter urging a more sober appreciation of the war. One of these was an officer of the British Regular Army—Major Francis Sainthill Anderson. Educated at Haileybury and Woolwich, Anderson served in France in 'Eagle Troop' Royal Horse Artillery, and commanded a battery of the Royal Field Artillery in Italy and France. He won the Military Cross and was killed in action, France, 25 August, 1918, at the age of twenty-three. He was only twenty-one when he wrote this letter. The failure of his prophecy— no war in the next generation—does not detract from his convictions.

Late evening of 6 November [1916].

To his Mother.

. . . I now go farther still in my opinion of the War—I won't express it on paper, because being a soldier by profession it would not be considered suitable. Your attitude is *wrong* like everyone else's at home, who doesn't realize it. If people would cease to be stupidly casual and untruthful when on leave, and let people know the truth—you for one would very soon alter your opinion. Europe is mad and no one realizes it.

Don't you realize that Socialists will rule the world after this War, and who are greater pacifists than the Socialists? Then consider the power of Socialism in Germany and remember that *all* the manhood of Germany has seen this War—it is foolish to prate about another War in the next generation, but I can't express myself forcibly and convincingly when my strongest arguments are not put forward.

This isn't War as the world understands the word at all. The truth of the matter is everyone out here considers it only fair to one's womankind to hush up the worst side of war, and make light of it—vide Bruce Bairnsfather [creator of the cartoon character 'Old Bill'] I don't find him nearly as funny as I used to.—No one can accuse me of having a dull sense of humour, but there are subjects one simply can't joke about. Mind you I am not under-going any horrors myself, which makes my arguments all the more unbiassed and valid! I have now got my own convictions, and I am not ashamed of them to anyone, though it may be unwise to express them—I think you will realize that up to now when on leave most of my statements about the war were sound, and my prophecies pretty accurate, though considered pessimistic by the 'Germany is on her last legs and will be brought to her knees next week' party.

You may remember I gave you a pretty shrewd idea about the Somme battle, long before it started. I won't burble on, as you probably think it's nonsense, besides there is no night shooting tonight, so I am going to have a damned good night.

Much love,
Saint.

Major Anderson took his battery to the Italian front in 1917 and at the French-Italian border had one of those amusing experiences which happen at times to all soldiers and which punctuate the boredom and the carnage. He wrote to his mother on 12 December, 1917.

One night on the train journey, just about 12 midnight, we

77

stopped at a station—I was naturally in my flea-bag—and the Railway Transport Officer woke me and told me that an Italian colonel was on the platform, waiting to welcome me and any of my officers who cared to come. He said it was a thing not to be avoided, as it would cause offence, but I could come 'just as I was'. Thank the Lord I didn't take him too literally; I hopped out, pulled on a pair of slacks, muffler and coat, slipped my feet into unlaced shoes, and prepared to Entente. Met the Colonel who was most effusive and took me off as I thought to his private room to drink to the Allies: not a bit of it—he led me into a brightly lit up and crowded waiting room, with the remains of what looked like an alderman's banquet on the table. Crowds of ladies, soldiers of all nationalities, and civilians, all of whom stood up at once.

I have no recollection of ever having been so badly frightened before, during the whole war. I was led round and solemnly introduced to all these ladies, frightfully conscious of the disgusting conditions of my nails, hair, etc.—(we had been in the train six days, with poorish facilities for washing, and one is never at the top of one's form having been woken up at midnight!). I was then given the chair of honour and my embarrassing Ally filled glasses, rose, and made a flowery speech in French for my benefit! I was immensely relieved for a moment at getting out of the limelight, except that my embarrassment was increased by a constant flow of beauteous damsels, who gave me various flowers and flags symbolical of the Entente.

Then it dawned on me that I should have to answer that speech, and I felt very like seizing my hat and bolting—however, I duly rose, started in French, decided it wasn't worth the extra labour entailed, as only the colonel spoke French, and carried on in English. As I rose, everyone else stood up, too, which made matters worse. They tell me since that there was a Press representative there at this critical moment taking photographs—if I'd spotted him I should have intercepted my speech to throttle him! Having got off all the flowery stuff I could think of, I wound up by proposing 'le Roi d'Italie', had a frightful spasm for a moment that Italy was a republic after the recent troubles—recovered my composure and sat down exhausted.

We all trooped out to the train, taking individual farewells to everyone as we went out—I am convinced I shook hands cordially with the waitress, but I didn't mind by that time; I

might as well go the whole hog and be the eccentric foreigner.
I entertained thoughts of kissing the Colonel on both cheeks,
but realized the consequences would be too embarrassing for
the subalterns and everyone, so stamped stolidly out, and
nearly died of hysteria when I got back to the train. I laughed
the rest of the night without control—Lord I have never seen
anything so funny in my life.

9
'It seemed like a dream'

Unofficial truces, of the kind already described by two letter writers, were more common than official histories indicate. Usually they were initiated by the Germans so that wounded could be brought in. Captain D. S. Thompson, of Esquimalt, B.C., who had been a banker with the Niagara Falls branch of the Canadian Bank of Commerce, witnessed a truce on 3 March, 1917, following a British gas attack at Vimy, France.

12 March, 1917.

I was present at the truce in No Man's Land, arranged for the purpose of clearing the battlefield, and conversed with a German Regimental Commander, or Brigadier-General as he would be in our organization. He had arranged this with one of our battalion commanders on the morning of March 3rd, to last for two hours, from 10 a.m. to 12, and was held under the Red Cross flag. The German Brigadier claimed relationship to a Major Elliott, of the Royal Engineers, who was stationed at Esquimalt, B.C., before the war, and unfortunately, nobody present could deny his claim. He was loud in his praises of Major Travers Lucas, of Hamilton, who, he said, had led his men so gallantly right up to their wire. Apparently, it was not a common practice with their own officers. Both Colonel Beckett and Major Lucas lost their lives in this show. The German Brigadier was a Bavarian, and, to talk to, not a bad sort. He was educated at St. Paul's School in London and spoke perfect

English. He didn't like war, he said, and hoped it would soon be over, and mentioned how queer it would seem to go back to our different lines after the truce and 'pot at one another again'. These were his own words. Indeed, the whole affair seemed so queer, standing upright out there in broad daylight, without a shot being fired, that it seemed to most of us like a dream. Not a shot was fired for the rest of the day.

'*War is cruel and I detest it, but . . .*'

It might be thought that by April 1917 British soldiers would not still be writing with pride about the possibility of dying for their country. Yet such letters are commonplace and the following one is representative. It was written by a young Welshman, John Llewellyn Thomas Jones, educated at Llangollen County School. A printer before enlistment, Jones became a captain in the 3rd London Regiment and was killed in action, Flanders, 16 August, 1917, at the age of twenty-two.

4 April, 1917.

My Dearest Dad, Ethel and Gwen,
I have written this letter so that, in the event of anything happening to me, I do not go under without letting all you dear ones at home know how much I owe to your loving care and the little kindnesses that go to make life so pleasant and inviting.

You know what an undemonstrative nature mine is, but my love for you all is, nevertheless, strong and deep, and though I said nothing about these things before I left England, it was just because I couldn't—my heart was too full.

One has to face the prospect of getting knocked out, as many other and probably better fellows than I have been. All I can say is that you do not grieve for me, because, although it may sound exceedingly quixotic, how better can one make one's exit from this world than fighting for the country which has sheltered and nurtured one all through life?

War is cruel and I detest it, but since it was not possible to keep out of this without loss of prestige and perhaps worse, it behoves us all to carry it on to a successful conclusion. Of course, it entails sacrifices, but that is all in the game. I had hoped to be able to return home and take up what little responsibility lay in my power away from your shoulders and to care for and look after the girls, but if that is not to be, I want you all to remember that though the break may seem unbearable—there are many other homes which have suffered losses. We should rather, I think, thank God that we have been a happy and united little family. I know how hard it is, and, as I write, the thought that I may not see you dear ones again in this world brings a lump to my throat and the tears to my eyes. I trust that I shall return, but . . .

All I can say to you is that I thank God for giving me the best father in the world and two very dear sisters. I cannot write to all, but send my deepest love to ——— I don't think that I can write any more, so just good-bye and God bless you all and protect you is my fervent prayer.

With all my fondest love,
Yours affectionately,
Llew.

'It's a Christian thing, and a British thing'

Young Captain Jones had simple, uncomplicated ideals, but in mid-1917 older Englishmen with equally clear but more profound idealism were joining the forces. Sense of duty must have been profound indeed to take a Public School headmaster into the Army at the age of forty-one. He was Harry Sackville Lawson, educated at Haileybury and Peterhouse, Cambridge, and later appointed Headmaster of Buxton College. He joined the Royal Field Artillery as a lieutenant towards the end of the summer term of 1917 and from France wrote a letter to his former pupils. It is a sermon, a self-justification, a homily—all in one. But most of all it is a highly professional lesson and for me, personally, it is one of the most significant letters to have survived the Great War. Unfortunately, Mr Lawson did not survive—he was killed in action on 5 February, 1918. We can be sure he met his end with the dignity he tried to inculcate in his pupils.

France, 3 July, 1917.

My dear Boys.

I wish I could be with you in person to say good-bye to you all, and to hand over my Headmastership to my successor. Instead,

I'm writing from a dug-out, to the sound of guns, the sort of message I want you to have before Term ends. But although I am in a dug-out at the front, I am picturing myself as sitting in my study at the College in the midst of surroundings of busy boyhood. I see the war potato field and the cricket pitch—the wickets casting a dark shadow in glaring contrast with the thin, white line of the block. Momentarily I think of the need of camouflage for concealing the position from the observation of hostile aircraft. Only for the moment. I'm back again in the study, and a bell, rather jaded and weary, has sounded the end of a period.

I've got one thing in particular to say to you all—just the main thing we've talked about together in its different bearings in the past—just the one important thing which keeps life sweet and clean and gives us peace of mind. It's a Christian thing, and it's a British thing. It's what the Bible teaches—it's what the Christian martyrs suffered in persecution for. It soon found root in England and began not only to fill the land, but also to spread abroad and become the heritage of the Empire. It's the story of the Crusaders, of the Reformation, of the downfall of the power of Spain, of our colonization, of the destruction of Napoleon's might, of the abolition of slavery, and of the coming awakening of Germany. The thing is this: Playing the game for the game's sake.

Now I've had many opportunities in years gone by of having a talk with you about this, and I've always found that we've got a clear starting-off point. For whether I have been talking to a boy alone, or to a class in its class-room, or to the school met together in the New Hall, I have found opinion quite clear and quite decided as to what the game is and what the game is not. We've had a sure foundation. And the difficulty for us all consists, not in knowing what the game is, but in trying to live up to the standard of life which our knowledge of the game puts before us. Don't think that I am referring to the breaking of school rules. I am not. School rules don't live for ever, and, further, school rules suffer change. I am referring to deeper things than these, to rules which do live for ever and which do not suffer change. I am thinking of high honesty of purpose and of the word duty.

I'm going to tell you a story of something that happened at the College in days, I think, not within the memory of any of you. I pick this story because it illustrates well what I have said about school rule and deeper rule.

On a certain whole school day afternoon in the Lent Term some years ago, the Vth Form made a raid upon the IVth Form. The IVth barricaded themselves very securely in their own class-room by piling up desks and furniture against both doors. The raid was still in progress when I came along at half-past three to take the IVth in English. I passed through the IIIrd, where there were evident symptoms of excitement, and came to the door of the IVth. The door wouldn't open. But my voice acting as a kind of 'Sesame', the barricade was quickly removed and I entered. The class-room was pandemonium, desks littering the place in wild confusion, and in particular concentrated against the door opposite to that through which I had entered. I held a court of enquiry—pronounced judgment —went to the study for my cane and dealt with the IVth Form ringleaders on the spot. This mind you, for a breach of school rule. Desks are not designed to be used for splinterproof dug-outs. Now the enquiry showed clearly that though the IVth were guilty, they were not nearly so guilty as the Vth. So peace once more reigning in the IVth, I went along to the new hall to have a talk with the Vth. I told them what had happened—what punishment had been meted out to the IVth, and I said, 'You've got the IVth into a row and you are the guiltier party of the two. I have caned the principal culprits in the IVth, and I shall be in the study at five o'clock and shall be glad to cane there those of you who feel you ought to turn up.'

At five o'clock seven of them arrived and received their caning. Before they left I said to them, 'I'm very proud of you chaps, and I've got to thank you for the first caning I've ever enjoyed giving.'

' *The Flying Corps are mighty warriors*'

During 1916 and 1917 the air war had been intensive and dog-fights were common above the battlefields. The planes were flimsy, the pilots gallant and the casualties many. Fights took place at relatively low altitudes, so there were thousands of onlookers; also the fliers could see every detail of the battle-field. During the early days of the Royal Flying Corps most pilots were army officers who had transferred. One of them was

Lieutenant Walter Bertram Wood, Hampshire Regiment and
R.F.C., who twice won the Military Cross. His brother,
Second-Lieutenant Edwin Leonard Wood, 1st Royal Scots
Fusiliers, in a letter to their father, draws a vivid contrast
between the airman's attitude to war and the soldier's attitude.

16 September, 1917.

I am glad to hear you were able to visit Bert [Walter] in his
native haunts and see him fly. Dorothy [Edwin's wife] tells me
that you got his official record and it pans out at thirty-six
machines smashed and brought down. [Walter had been in
combat thirty-six times but in fact had brought down eighteen
enemy planes: this ranks him seventy-fourth among British air
aces of the Great War.] That is good work for three months. . . .
If I could account for just so many individual Boches in the
time I should feel happier. However, my chances hitherto have
been none too rosy; before the leaves fall they will have
improved (D.V.). The Flying Corps are mighty warriors; they
do their business in the light of all eyes, and show as much regard
for Johnny's 'Archies' [anti-aircraft shells] as they do for the
distant stars. Beneath their aerial antics, the infantry moil and
trudge and fire, no one looks on, no one applauds.

The man with the bowed back, slinging eternal shovelfuls of
clay out the slowly growing hole, stops, draws his seamed hand
across his sweating brow, tilts back the irksome steel hat, and
looks up at the great, flat-winged bird with eyes that have
looked on bitter things, and applauds in his uncouth way. Our
stage is a rough one; last week we doubled and crawled
alternately some one thousand yards over a battlefield, on which
it was literally impossible to walk between shell holes—there is
no 'between holes'. It is all one big, puckered grin—a sarcastic
smile on the troubled face of Mother Earth, half incredulous
that men could do such things. Still the airman sails serenely up
yonder, fearing nothing—and we go surging below.

Edwin, aged twenty-four and married, could be objective and
comparative. Walter, only nineteen, was full of subjective
enthusiasm for this new form of warfare. 'Ye gods, what a
life!' he wrote to his father in April 1917. 'It is composed of
vivid excitement and super-luxuriant ease, and mark my words,

85

it is a topping combination.' Yet he could write to his mother, 2 November, 1917, 'I know what it is you are wanting to know the whole time, Mummie: "Is that dear little sugar and butter son's cold any better?" Yes, Mummie, it is. I have spent two days in bed, and am just about fit again, so don't worry.' He died in a flying accident a week later. Edwin was killed in action, Flanders, 27 September, 1917, aged twenty-four.

' I was inclined to shut my eyes and run'

When the Great War broke out Philip Russell Keightley was a student at Trinity College, Dublin, with a shy love of literature —which he was studying—and a genius for friendship. He became a second-lieutenant in the Royal Garrison Artillery and did not reach the front until September 1916, spending that winter and the greater part of 1917 in the Ypres salient. In the autumn of that year he was transferred to the Somme. Now a captain, he had decided to make the Army his career, despite his evident horror and distress at what he saw during a duty which took him across the battlefield. Keightley survived the war but died of illness while on leave, February 1919, aged twenty-four.

28 November, 1917.

Addressee unknown.

I have been trying to finish this letter for the last three days, but have really never had more than ten minutes' rest. After our latest captures, batteries have had to be pushed on and observation posts advanced. I thought I had already seen something of war, but from 4 o'clock a.m. on the 26th till yesterday at 6 p.m. I have seen all I ever want to see again. I do not care to dwell on it, and I cannot describe my experience. That would need the brutal realism of Zola.

It happened like this. On the 26th my group had to establish an advanced observation post at a late Hun strong point, some four hundred yards behind the front line—perhaps I should say the yawning series of shell-holes which constitute the front line. Naturally we had to have a line laid out, and though it was not my job to see to it personally, I thought it best to see it laid down under my own eyes.

At 4 a.m. I started off for our present observation post, and walked up from Group H.Q., cadging a lift on a transport carrying up rations for men and guns, till I reached a point where I had to leave the road and strike across country. I passed first through the area of heavy batteries—once our observation post area, which I know so well—and then across last year's No Man's Land and the old Hun line now occupied by the R.F.A. This ground, too, was familiar to me from many a weary vigil. Then I went on up the slope to the first ridge through the shell-holes, remains of trenches, pill boxes, strong points, and—smells—faint at first, but more poignant as I got further forward. At last I reached our observation post, but was too late to start work before dusk. The observation post is an old Hun dug-out, and one can judge from its massive strength and comfort that he intended to stay here, and to stay indefinitely.

It was too dark to see anything of what was going on in front, so I made myself comfortable in one of the bunks, smoked a pipe, and wondered how many Hun officers had done exactly the same a few weeks before; and whether these officers were as tired of the war as I was, or settled into the bunk with as many wishes for a quiet night. As a matter of fact, I had a quiet night. The Major who was manning the observation post was a very keen fellow, and though I offered to relieve him he would not hear of it, and declined my services. So I slept the sleep of the just with a quiet conscience till 7 o'clock. Having breakfasted on tea (minus milk), bread (minus butter), sardines and bully—an excellent meal—I started off to lay my line. Everything was quiet in the grey, solemn light. The only moving thing I saw was a party or two of stretcher-bearers, with their pitiful burden, trudging back along a trench to a dressing station, a mile or so in the rear, and a few more, led by a padre, carrying their stretchers and going forward on their noble errand.

I carried my line across the shell-holes to this track, and, as the going was easier, followed it on. How I wished I had not! I had gone about two hundred yards down the track when my sense of smell warned me of what was coming. Here were a couple of horses possibly three days dead, and then I stumbled on all that remained of what was once a German—and another—and another—in awful and rapid succession. I thought of leaving the road, but found the going too heavy in the shell-holes—remember I had my wire to carry—so I was forced to come back upon the track. I will not continue to describe the sights I saw, but at one spot the road for about a hundred and fifty yards was literally paved deep—I do not exaggerate—with German dead, ghastly, mutilated, contorted. I noticed a few khaki-clad figures here and there. I cannot tell you how glad I was to reach my destination—an old farm house, concreted and loop-holed—and find stimulus and refreshment in my flask.

On my way back I kept off that road, but found the cross-country route nearly as bad. I passed Englishmen and Germans side by side in eternal amity—some half-buried in the open, some whose only distinguishing mark was an arm or a leg and a crowd of flies. Heaps of equipment, rifles, ammunition, bombs, rations, broken and blood stained stretchers, were scattered everywhere. I was inclined to shut my eyes and run, but by keeping my imagination well in hand and thinking about nothing but the shortest and safest way back I got to my quarters quite safely, perspiration streaming off me, a very empty feeling in my stomach, and a very weak feeling in my knees. Not at all a hero, I was once more guilty of breaking the pledge with very weak rum and water.

My adventures did not end here. In the afternoon one of our batteries had to do a shoot on a target which was rather close to our infantry line, so I set out for Battalion H.Q. to warn them. By this time I had found the best way, and my journey was not too unpleasant. As I was coming back, however, the Hun thought fit to put down a barrage, and by good fortune I got right into the middle of it. For fifteen minutes I saw all my past life float before my eyes. I anathematized the size of my tin helmet, wondering if it would stop a 5.9 [a 5.9-inch shell] and thought how great the chances were of a shell dropping right into the hole in which I was cowering. It was not a pleasant position. Yet, when it was all over, I decided I would much rather face that ordeal a second time than have to lay that wire down the road of death again. Travelling over that ground where shell-hole touched shell-hole, I could not help wondering how men had ever lived through it as our glorious infantry had, and, watching the Hun barrage, I thought what a hell it had been. Yet, coming back at night, I met a wounded officer, who talked about it as 'a lovely scrap', and I think his enthusiasm was genuine—for the moment.

Letters from the Front

'*Just for the beautiful poetry of it all*'

In December 1914 Captain Claude Templer, educated at Wellington College and the Royal Military Academy, Sandhurst, was wounded and taken prisoner. He escaped late in 1917 and rejoined his regiment, the Gloucestershires. In 1918 he took with him into battle the frustrations of his years of captivity and an heroic approach to war that was by now extremely rare among infantry officers. He was the 'worthy warrior' he had resolved to be and was killed in action 4 June, 1918, aged twenty-three.

France.
April, 1918.

Addressee unknown.

When I was locked up in Germany I used to pray for this moment; I used to dream of the romance of war, its wild strange poetry crept into my soul; I used to think that the glory of going back to the beautiful adventure was worth any price. And now it's all come true, just like things happen in fairy tales. I go into my dream country like a baby, eyes wide with wonder, ears strained to catch every note of the magic music I hear there. In my dream country is a piper like Hamelin's piper and I follow him. I follow into his cavern a spell-bound child, and I come out at the other end a warrior fully armed, longing for the day that my mettle shall be proved. And often I fail and then I must cross over to the dream country and I must drink romance from the music of the magic piper. And when I come out of the cavern again perhaps this time I *win*. The romance of war and love. That is what the music tells me. And I resolve to be a worthy warrior. To fight to the finish, to love to the finish, to sacrifice everything but never honour. And to do all this with no hope of payment, but as a volunteer, just for the beautiful poetry of it all.

10

'Aren't you sick of it, Fritz?'

Some of the best letters of the Great War came from the pen of Rowland Feilding, whose family had long been associated with the Coldstream Guards. Feilding was himself appointed captain in the 3rd Battalion Coldstream Guards in 1915. In 1916 he was given command, as a lieutenant-colonel, of the 6th Battalion Connaught Rangers and later of the 1st Civil Service Rifles. In 1929 Major-General Sir John Ponsonby said, 'How Feilding managed to survive the war will always remain a mystery to me and many others [especially] as he could not bear giving orders to a subordinate officer to carry out any dangerous duty and always managed to carry out the duty himself.' He won the Distinguished Service Order—little enough for the length and quality of his service. Feilding's letters, always frank and descriptive, and sometimes critical, were written to his wife, from whom he held back nothing.

Bethune.
7 August, 1915.

On my return from leave, on the 5th, I found the battalion just finishing a tour in the trenches in front of Cambrin, immediately south of the La Bassée road.

The trenches which the battalion was holding were new to us, and were very lively; and the contrast between the peaceful life I was leading with you and the children last Wednesday and my occupation the following day and night could scarcely have been greater. Nowhere along the whole front are the Germans and ourselves more close together than there. Twelve to fifteen yards was all that separated us in the advanced portions of the trench, and the ground between was a shapeless waste—a mass of mine-craters, including two so large that they are known officially as Etna and Vesuvius.

The ragged aspect of this advanced trench I cannot picture to you. The hundreds of bombs which explode in and around it each day and night have reduced it to a state of wild dilapidation that is indescribable. There is not a sandbag that is not torn to shreds, and the trench itself is half filled by the earth and debris that have dribbled down. So shallow and emaciated has this bit of trench now become that you have to stoop low or your head and shoulders poke above the parapet, and so near are you to the enemy that you have to move in perfect silence. The slightest visible movement brings a hail of bullets from the snipers, and the slightest sound a storm of hand-grenades.

The conditions are such that you cannot repair the damages as they should be repaired. You just have to do the best you can, with the result that when the tide of war has passed beyond these blood-soaked lines they will soon become obliterated and lost among the wilderness of craters. The tripper who will follow will pass them by, and will no doubt pour out his sentiment on the more arresting concrete dug-outs and the well-planned earthworks of the reserve lines well behind.

I did a bit of bombing myself during the thirty hours I was there—a rather different occupation to our tea-party in the grotto at Rainhill! Who would have imagined, two years ago, that I should actually so soon be throwing bombs like an anarchist?

Tommy Robartes's [Captain the Hon. T. Agar-Robartes, M.P.; died of wounds 30 September, 1915] Company has a band, and, the night before my arrival, being the anniversary of the declaration of war, he tried a 'ruse de guerre'. The band was posted in a sap [a type of trench] leading from the fire-trench, and, at six minutes to midnight, opened with 'Die Wacht am Rhein'. It continued with 'God Save the King' and 'Rule Britannia', each tune being played for two minutes. Then, as the last note sounded, every bomber in the battalion, having been previously posted on the fire-step, and the grenade-firing rifles, trench-mortars, and bomb-throwing machine, all

shock it would be to them! But we must see it through. All are agreed upon that.

Nine of my best officers went over yesterday. Three of these are left today. And, in addition, one more of my Company Commanders (Fitzgerald) is gone, as the result of this enterprise. He was wounded while cutting the gaps through our own wire, preparatory to the raid, so severely that he too may die.

But all this is not unusual. It is the toll to be expected from a raid when it is unsuccessful, and indeed often when it is successful: and the success or failure of a raid is largely a matter of chance.

I was present at the burial of some of the killed this afternoon. including that of two of my most promising young officers. That is the tragedy of the war. The best are taken. The second best are often left in the safe places.

General Pereira came and saw me this morning, and stayed some time. He was more kind and consoling than I can say.

Private Elwin, too, has died.

'Frightfulness is to be our watchword'

26 February, 1917.

There is a sequel to the affair of the 19th. [Feilding refers to an unofficial and quite spontaneous armistice between his own men and the Germans confronting them so that wounded could be brought in.] It has been suggested that the so-called 'armistice' constituted a breach of the order which forbids fraternization. The incident unfortunately occurred right on the top of a memorandum dealing with the subject, and worded as follows:

1. A case has recently occurred in which the enemy are reported to have been allowed to approach our lines and remove the bodies of some of their dead.

Whilst doing this he was probably able to secure useful information as to the state of our wire and the ground in its vicinity, and in any case he was permitted to deprive us of what may have been a valuable identification.

2. The Divisional Commander wishes it to be clearly understood by all ranks that any understanding with the enemy of this or any other description is strictly forbidden.

94

We have to deal with a treacherous and unscrupulous foe, who, from the commencement of the present war, has repeatedly proved himself unworthy of the slightest confidence. No communication is to be held with him without definite instructions from Divisional Headquarters, and any attempt on his part to fraternize with our own troops is to be instantly repressed.

3. Commanding Officers are to take steps to ensure that all ranks under their command are acquainted with these instructions.

In the event of any infringement of them, disciplinary action is to be taken.

As a matter of fact I had not seen this memorandum, which arrived when I was away from the battalion. God knows whether I should have acted differently had I done so! Anyway, a Court of Enquiry is to be convened, to decide whether we did fraternize or not, and orders still more stringent than that which I have quoted have been issued.

In future, if fifty of our wounded are lying in Noman's Land, they are (as before) to remain there till dark, when we may get them in if we can; but no assistance, tacit or otherwise, is to be accepted from the enemy. Ruthlessness is to be the order of the day. Frightfulness is to be our watchword. Sportsmanship, chivalry, pity—all the qualities which Englishmen used to pride themselves in possessing—are to be scrapped.

In short, our methods henceforth are to be strictly Prussian; those very methods to abolish which we claim to be fighting this war. And all because the enemy took toll for his generosity the other day. [The Germans had 'arrested' a young British officer who had gone, armed, to the German trenches and looked into them while the armistice was in progress.]

'To laugh or to cry'

Near Ervillers.
8 October, 1917.

. . . The section of front line which I hold is, as I have told you, more or less of a graveyard. Many soldiers lie buried in the parapet, and in some cases their feet project into the trench. The positions are marked, where known. We come across others,

promptly, which might prove dangerous;—and that is what happened this morning.

The double sentries on duty in the sunken road heard, but in the darkness did not see, a movement in front of them. Hesitating to shoot, they challenged. The immediate reply was a volley of hand-grenades. Private Mayne, who had charge of the Lewis gun, was hit 'all over' in many parts, including the stomach. His left arm was reduced to pulp. Nevertheless, he struggled up, and leaning against the parapet, with his uninjured hand discharged a full magazine [forty-seven rounds] into the enemy, who broke, not a man reaching our trench. Then he collapsed and fell insensible across his gun.

The second sentry's foot was so badly shattered that it had to be amputated in the trench. The doctor has just told me that he performed this operation without chloroform, which was unnecessary owing to the man's numbed condition, and that while he did it the man himself looked on, smoking a cigarette, and with true Irish courtesy thanked him for his kindness when it was over.

Words cannot express my feelings of admiration for Private Mayne's magnificent act of gallantry, which I consider well worthy of the V.C. It is, however, improbable that he will live to enjoy any decoration that may be conferred upon him.

Feilding expected high-level acknowledgment of the successful and heroic repulse of the German raiders by Private Mayne and his companion. Instead he received a memo which had been circulated throughout the Division. *Another instance has occurred of an enemy patrol reaching within bombing distance of our line. This must not occur again. Our patrols must meet the enemy patrols boldly in Noman's Land.* . . . Frustrated and bitter, Feilding wrote to his wife, 'How simple and grand it all sounds! I think I can see the writer, with his scarlet tabs [the insignia of a staff officer] seated in his nice office 7 or 8 miles behind the line, penning this pompous admonition.' [Private Mayne died of his wounds and received only a posthumous mention in dispatches; this would have entitled him, had he lived, to wear a miniature bronze oak leaf on the ribbon of his Victory Medal. In the British Army the only posthumous distinctions at that time were a mention in dispatches, the lowest award, and the

Victoria Cross, the highest. Hence many brave men went unrewarded for their finest hour. Even today the only additional award which can be won posthumously is the George Cross.

'Lord! How I hate the system!'

> *Auchel, Pas de Calais.*
> *17 September, 1918.*

. . . I have spent the day intensively, writing up the official narrative of the recent fighting, which, thankfully, I have now finished, as well as the recommendations for awards—that thankless and most difficult of all the duties, apart from the heavy work of rebuilding the battalion, which falls to a Battalion Commander after every battle.

Honours are not, as you might logically suppose, awarded in bulk to a battalion, in proportion to its merit, and left to the Colonel and his Brigadier to distribute in such manner as they think fit. Would that they were! No. They have to be dragged out of the Higher Authorities like back teeth. In each individual recommendation a 'specific act' must be cited, which, if there is to be any chance of favourable consideration, must be made to 'stand out'.

It must be couched in the flamboyant language of the Penny Dreadful, and the result often is that the most deserving cases get cut out by the Authorities, far behind the line, whose function it is to decide these matters, and who, as a rule, have no personal or first-hand knowledge of the men or the conditions upon which they pass judgment.

It has been said that the pen is mightier than the sword, and I can truthfully say that, under our system, if a battalion is to get its proper share of honours, it is essential that the Commander should have at his disposal—not necessarily a truthful but at least a flowery pen. No matter how brilliant the performance, it must be dressed up in language which would startle the performer—generally a modest man—could he see it, so gaudily must the lily be painted. Apropos of which a story is told of a certain C.O. who once recommended one of his men for a Military Medal [the junior award for bravery]. The recommendation was turned down, the 'story', presumably, not being considered good enough.

The C.O. was disappointed, since the case was a particularly

I I

'We need women who are shameless in their pity'

In the last year or so of the war a young British artillery officer, on leave in Paris, met and fell in love with an American Red Cross girl. He wrote her a series of letters, none of which he ever posted because, as he said in one of the letters, 'What right have I, who may be dead within a month, to speak to you of love?' At another point, he wrote, 'If I live perhaps some day when war is ended you will receive all your mail at once.' He secreted the bundle of letters in a dug-out of a gun position which was later found badly damaged and abandoned. The officer-writer was presumably killed. The letters gave no indication of his name or unit and the name of the girl he loved was not mentioned. The officer who found the letters took them to John Lane, the publisher, who printed them in 1919, partly in the hope that the girl concerned would claim her letters. She never did.

> The mail has just come in. It was brought up on the ammunition limbers. We heard the cry, 'Mail up!', and then the running feet of the men. It's queer to think how far those letters travel and how safely they arrive. They are brought up to us under shell-fire, through gas, by runners, pack animals, limbers. Since no movement is allowed near the guns by day, they invariably reach us at night. Before ever they can be distributed the ammunition has to be unloaded so that the teams may get out of range. That accounts for the speed with which

the men work. They form a chain, and pass the shells swiftly to the gun-pits. Until everything is safely stored away the pages from their mothers, wives and sweethearts must wait. When the last shell has been laid in its rack, they scramble to the sergeant-major's dug-out. He crouches over the bag by the light of the candle and reads aloud the name on each envelope or parcel. Finally the bag is empty. He turns it upside down and shakes it. There will be no more news from home till next night. The crowd scatters; the blackness becomes again lonely.

We officers have to sit still and wait for our letters to be brought to us by our servants. It's a sore trial to our patience—part of the price we pay for our rank. Tonight I made sure I should hear from you. At the cry, 'Mail up!' I forsook my dignity and went out on the pretence of seeing that the teams were clear of the position. It was such a night; the stars and snow were like silver inlaid in ebony. From the gun-pits came the glow of fires. Men were already sitting round them in silence, reading by the light of the jumping flames. The frost on the duck-board crackled beneath my tread. War seemed to have ceased for a little while; for a little while memories travelled back to affections and quiet.

My servant met me with a bundle of letters. 'The officers'. Will you take them, sir?'

I returned to the hole in the ground which we call our mess, and sorted them out on the table. At a glance I saw that there was nothing from you—my three letters were in known handwritings. A queer way to tell! You mean more to me than anyone in the world, yet I have never seen your handwriting. That brings home to me vividly how much we are strangers.

Every one in our mess has something tonight. Jack Holt has made the biggest haul; there are four from his wife. He married her in a hurry two years ago. He'd only known her a week, I understand. They had a four days' honeymoon; then he came to France. He's spent about thirty days with her in his entire life. I never knew a man more in love with anybody; I'm his best pal, so he tells me about her. Our major got only one letter. His girl is, like you, in a French hospital. I have an idea that she plays him up sometimes. It's incredible that anyone should trifle with our major. He doesn't look very pleased; he's puckering his brows. Then there's Bill Lane: he didn't come off so badly. He's a nervous kind of chap and, despite that, plucky.

Rapoport, aged twenty-four, educated at Tonbridge School and New College, Oxford, found a more positive love than the unknown gunner and became engaged while on leave in England. Returning to his regiment, the Rifle Brigade, Rapoport wrote excitedly to his fiancée.

6 May 1918.

The mail has just come in and I've got 14 letters! Among them, my darling, were 5 from you. So you can imagine what I feel like. I got the very first one of all tonight, the one you sent to me at Havre. They've been awfully slack in forwarding it. . . . Darling, you were splendid when you saw me off at Waterloo. You just typified the women of England by your attitude, everything for us men, and you have your dark times to yourselves so as not to depress us. . . . You mean so much to me, you have no idea how much. Life without you would be absolutely empty. I wonder how ever I got on before. As a matter of fact I am full of love and for the last 2 or 3 years I've had a longing to pour it out on someone, and I've always lived in the hope of doing so—that kept me going. Now I've got someone on whom I can and *have* lavished *all* my love.

My darling, I love and adore you from the bottom of my heart. You wait till I come home—you will get some kisses then, and I shall hold you tight—you know how, my darling, don't you . . .?

I am so glad we both are alike on the question of friends. Of course I want you to carry on with your men friends just as if I didn't exist. One thing I am sure of as that I exist, that is that I have all your heart and all your love. So I just want you to enjoy yourself—I love you so much. Have a topping time on the river and at shows, etc., with your friends, won't you. I asked W.W. to write to me still though we were engaged—just as friends. I feel very sorry for your friends. Just impress on them that you can be chums just as before. I know it isn't quite the same, but I should like it, because I know what a help you'd be to any man. Just thank your friends for their good wishes, will you? Oh, the more I think of it, the more I realize how lucky I am in having you for my *own* darling wife-to-be. Oh, hasn't God been good to me—far more than I deserve.

On 17 May Lieutenant Rapoport concluded a letter to his

sweetheart: 'If my —— prays for her boy, I feel somehow that
God will listen to her prayers an awful lot. . . .' Two weeks later
he was posted missing during the violent third battle of the
Aisne and his body was never found.

'*I should not change places with anyone*'

The Allied attacks were gaining impetus by August 1918 and
there were positive signs that German resistance was crumbling.
But all Allied soldiers knew by now the cost of recapturing
territory and there is a sense of premonition in the letter
written by Lieutenant Hedley John Goodyear, of 102nd
Battalion, Canadian Expeditionary Force. A schoolteacher,
Goodyear was killed in action the next day when he took part
in the British attack on a six-mile front between the Ancre and
Somme rivers.

21 August, 1918.

Dearest Mother,
This is the evening before the attack and my thoughts are with
you all at home. But my backward glance is wistful only
because of memories and because of the sorrow which would
further darken your lives tomorrow.

With hope for mankind and with visions of a new world a
blow will be struck tomorrow which will definitely mark the
turn of the tide. It will be one of a grand series of victories which
will humble the selfish and barbarous foeman and will exalt the
hearts that are suffering for freedom.

I have no misgivings for myself in tomorrow's encounter. It
does not matter whether I survive or fall. A great triumph is
certain and I shall take part in it. I shall strike a blow for freedom along with thousands of others who count personal safety as
nothing when freedom is at stake. In a few moments I shall
make the final address to my men and shall strengthen their
hearts, if they need strengthening, with the language of men of
war! We shall strive only to achieve victory. We shall not hold
our own lives dear.

The hour is all more dramatic for me because for the first
time since I came to France I am close to the spot consecrated by

the blood of our gallant dead. It was here that noble Raymond fell and Joe and Kenneth shed their blood in freedom's cause. I trust to be as faithful as they. I do not think for a moment that I shall not return from the field of honour but in case I should not, give my last blessing to Father and my greatest thanks for all he did for me. Give my blessing to Roland and his family and to the others that survive me. I have no regrets and no fear of tomorrow. I should not change places with anyone in the world just now except General Foch [the Allied Commander-in-Chief]. I shall be my father's and mother's son tomorrow again. God bless you all.

Hedley.

'*A passionate faith in my fellow men*'

Lieutenant Henry Lamont Simpson had a feeling and understanding for men far beyond his twenty-one years. Educated at Pembroke College, Cambridge, he gave 'poet' as his occupation and his work was published posthumously in 1919. He wrote this letter shortly before his death in action in France, 29 August, 1918, while serving with the Lancashire Fusiliers.

Addressee unknown.

The more I see of men, the more I love them. A common song (even now and then a dirty song) can make one glad and sad beyond words, because one has heard men singing it times out of number. In all seriousness, the cheap popular songs of the last few years can move me infinitely more than the divinest music, because of the men I have heard sing them. This is not merely a sentimental lingering over dead friendships and individual passions—that element is very small. The main thing is a love for, a passionate faith in, my fellow men. I believe with all my heart that man is, in the main, a lovable, and, at bottom, a good creature. (Curse the word good! but you know what I mean—worthy, sterling, right, true, real.) He sings dirty songs and swears, and is altogether a sensual drunken brute at times; but get to know him, start by loving him, believe in him through thick and thin, and you will not go unrewarded.

I am aware that this is chaotic, illogical, and possibly, to the worldly wise, BOSH. But it is a belief that was struggling in me even at school, that flowered forth in the Army in England, and that bore fruit in France. It is part of me, the best part of me, and right or wrong I shall stick to it. (The right or wrong is for your benefit—I *know* I am right.) And because of this, furiously, I *want* to write—to let everybody know it; and for the first time in my life I absolutely cannot write a line. I have not yet arrived at 'recollecting in tranquillity'. I am too much sizzling with belief to be coherent. [Wordsworth wrote that poetry is emotion recollected in tranquillity.]

12
'America can't imagine the terrible realities'

The United States entered the war on 6 April, 1917, and partly because American soldiers did not experience the spirit of the years 1914, 1915 and 1916 their letters are quite unlike those of their allies. Collectively they can make monotonous reading because they lack reflection and thought, though to compensate they have an engaging breeziness. A dominant theme is what American bayonets will do to German bellies; another is inefficiency in the Army and defeatism at home. Another fair generalization is that American letters are more sentimental and less sensitive than British letters. The more interesting and philosophic correspondence is from officers, as with the British. The selection which follows shows several facets of the American soldier's character.

Houston Woodward, born 2 February, 1896, was one of those Americans who volunteered for service before their own country entered the war. He served in the American Ambulance, a volunteer unit attached to the French Army, and quickly became disenchanted about the adventure of war. He wrote to his father early in May 1917.

> Sherman's remark about war was only half right. I wish I would never hear another shell. People used to come into this war for adventure. This war isn't adventure, it's a dirty, stinking, rotten, nasty hell. There can't be a man living that likes it who

110

has seen it close. Lots of things we read in the American papers are screamingly funny, but pitiable in their ignorance of what war really is. Even the Parisians don't know what it's like and America can't possibly imagine the terrible realities. The Consul General was here the other day, and said he would feel safer in the trenches than crossing the Champs Elysees. Poor fool! That's the most asinine remark I've ever heard. He was itching to see the trenches. You couldn't pay me or any other ambulanciers, or the French soldiers, to go near them if it wasn't our duty. I like the ambulance tremendously and would like to re-enlist, but feel it my duty to fight. Believe me, I don't want to fight and if I get killed I hope I kill at least fifty of those cochons first. It's terrible, the things they do. I'll believe any story I hear of them now. Is America making much heavy artillery? That's what's winning the war, for the British. They can't possibly make enough.

Woodward was referring to General William T. Sherman, the Union general noted for his march through Georgia, during the American Civil War, to subjugate the Confederate rebels. In August 1880 Sherman spoke to a big crowd in Columbus, Ohio: 'The war now is away back in the past and you [the veterans in the throng] can tell what books cannot. . . . There is many a boy here who looks on war as all glory, but, boys, it is all hell. You can bear this warning voice to generations yet to come.'

Woodward transferred to the French flying corps mainly because he was disillusioned by the low standard of Americans arriving as reinforcements. The risks of aerial warfare were as great as he explains in this letter to his mother, and he was killed in an unrecorded air action. The Germans buried him at Montdidier, where his grave was found in April 1918.

6 August, 1917.

Dear Mother :—

At last I feel I have time to write a letter long enough to let you know a bit about what has been going on recently.

In the first place, I severed diplomatic relations with the A.A. [American Army] July 23rd, and came to Avord July 24th. I wanted to stay in the section till August 19th, but found that if I did I could not get into French Aviation, so considered it useless and foolish to sacrifice aviation for three weeks of A.A. work in St. Menehould, where there is almost nothing doing, and since there were more than enough men in the section already. Since coming here my only regret has been that I did not leave the ambulance two weeks sooner . . . I have grown thoroughly disgusted with the ambulance. The crowd who have come over since America declared war are a wretched bunch of embusqués, have disgraced themselves and America in Paris, and are of no account at all.

Maybe you think by this that I regret my A.A. experience. Not a bit of it. I consider the time I served at the front the best I have ever lived. I shall always look back upon my A.A. life with the greatest of pleasure and satisfaction, but it grieves me terribly to see how the A.A. has gone to the dogs, recently. Enough on this subject.

And now I come to a subject, which, though not pleasant to talk about, must be met squarely in the face. I am now in aviation and all that that means. You haven't seen for yourself, so don't know, but I have seen and know. I don't want to scare you, and shall be as decent as possible about it, but it is only fair to tell you of the dangers, and after speaking of them this once we won't refer to them again. But just remember this war is the biggest thing so far in history, and no one in the world really has a right to refrain from doing his utmost, down to the giving up of his life. I may live through it all, of course, lots of aviators do, but an aviator's life isn't worth an awful lot the way things are done now. I prefer not to worry you more than I can help, however.

Some day when I am not so hot and sleepy I will write describing the school thoroughly. Just at present I'm getting so sleepy I don't see how I can possibly go on.

I get up at 4.15 every morning, attend flying class from six till eight, drill at 11.15, and fly again in the evening from 6.30 till 8.30. So far I have had about thirty sorties, or flights, in a dual control Caudron bi-plane, and now do all the work myself except the landing, which I will begin on tomorrow.

Am getting so awfully sleepy I can't go on any more, sorry, but will write soon again.

Am very well, but pretty tired owing to exceedingly irregular
eating and sleeping hours.

Very lovingly,
Houston.

'*The American Army needs roughnecks*'

Caspar Henry Burton Jr. was in England when war broke out,
and joined the 4th King's Regiment before transferring to the
Royal Fusiliers, in which he became a first-lieutenant. Most of
his letters were to his brother, a Jesuit priest in Massachusetts.
Burton died in 1920, from the delayed result of the wounds he
mentions in his letter, which is particularly interesting because
of his views on the needs of the American Army, then being
formed.

23 May, 1917.

Dear Spence,

I suppose the orthodox thing is to write to one's Father Con-
fessor before going into battle. As the next best thing I will write
now after stopping a Boche grenade; principally because I can
do nothing else but write. They won't let me lie down in bed
and there is nothing to read. Well, I cut things a bit fine this
time. A German gentleman who we failed to 'mop up' en
passant (we didn't miss many), as his last act on this earth
soaked me in the back with a small grenade and as near as I can
make out, by all rights I should be pushing up the daisies, but
'I ain't', and what's more, I have every intention of getting
O.K. again. In fact, I may get in for the last three or four years
of the war, but will be out for some months now. Read the
accounts of the fighting on Sunday, May 20th, and you will
know what we did. We are all pretty chesty [proud] in the old
Division. I shall never forget early Sunday morning in the quiet
with my picked crew of bruisers waiting for the hour. And then
in one second every hellish device yet invented all going at
once. I had just about forty minutes of it before I got mine. But
I don't think I shall ever forget a single incident. It was what
we are always praying for, a hand-to-hand scrap (a heavy fog
did away with the M. guns). I will tell you about it at some
future date.

113

My point is this. What the American Army needs is 'rough-necks', thousands and thousands of them. Rub this in and keep rubbing it in. People of culture are needed in small doses, but 'hard guys' are the thing. For instance, the following is the composition of the selected party under me which led the attack Sunday:

Private Wallace, a stoker in civil life.

Private Put, a boilermaker.

Sergeant Malloy, a regular soldier, who has been sentenced to be shot once, for being drunk on active service and reduced to the ranks six times.

Private Astin, my servant, plays a fiddle in a cheap dance hall.

Private Casey, owns a small 'pub' in Cork.

Private Hard, a carter.

Private Michaels, a collier.

Private Hatnough, I think is a burglar, but my evidence is only indirect.

Corp. Lopez, a halfbreed Portugee gentleman of the sea.

Sergeant Gallagher, a Liverpool policeman, etc., etc.,—just thirty picked men.

My point is that we are the kind that were picked, and when you get a lot like this seeing red, you don't need much leader-ship. No sir, Sir Galahads are not of much use against the Hun.

I am wondering if, after some months light duty or some-thing of the sort, whether they could use me as an instructor in the Harvard O.T.C. I could get leave to go there, I am sure, in case I am unfit for active service again. Of course, I am in wonderful condition and may be able to get well enough in a few months to get out here again, but they tell me that lung wounds are the slowest of the lot.

Love,

Cap.

Lambert Wood, a twenty-two-year-old lieutenant from Port-land, Oregon, had much the same idea as Burton when he wrote to his family on 4 November, 1917. 'This war is not going to be won by YMCA workers or relief societies or Red Cross workers but by two-fisted fighting men, six feet tall and wearing size 10 shoes, who can fight and work for 18 hours, eat a huge meal and get up and do it all over again.' A month later he wrote a letter of interesting contrast—martial vehemence and personal gentleness.

7 December, 1917.

Dearest folks,

Well, Monday was a happy day for the officers [at a school Wood was attending]. We got a sack of mail—the first for three weeks. I got ten letters, nine from home and one from my girl. Do you know, I really must be in love, for I opened her letter first. I am very, very happy that you folks are all so well and working so hard. I laughed when you wondered if the big harvest moon was looking down on me. It probably was, but I had somewhat the feeling of the man in one of Bairnsfather's cartoons.

I am very happy in my work. My captain and myself are great friends. . . . Let me tell you this, we can beat the Boche to a frazzle if we go into this with heart and soul. If you ever hear of any calamity howlers, squelch them for being traitors. We can beat the Boche only by fighting, and we are better fighters and better killers than the Boche. There is no pessimism in the American Army over here but we must have the support, moral and material, of the folks at home! Our killing spirit must be aroused but it is rising and Lord! I hope I am in the drive when it comes—when the Americans bloody their bayonets! . . . But just keep in mind the people who are shouting calamity are pro-German and traitors. . . . Prepare for years more and do things thoroughly. We are fighting a nation that is as bad as its individual soldiers, who sham death and then shoot the soldiers in the stomachs who pass over them. Try to spread the gospel among your friends. I believe it is the truth, as I have done all in my power to find out the situation. I always was an inquisitive cuss.

Oh yes, I guess I am in love with M—— S——, my first real affair. She seems to care for me, thank the Lord! and some day, if I live, I will ask her to marry me. I am very happy and hope she loves me—but don't know. She may just feel sorry for me and I am no object of pity.

Wood refers to one of Captain Bruce Bairnsfather's best-known cartoons. A drawing shows a woman leaning from her bedroom window and looking at the full moon as she says, 'And to think that it's the same dear old moon that's looking down on *him*!' A second drawing shows a wiring party at work in front of the trenches, as 'Old Bill', the artist's famous character, looks at the moon and says, 'This blinkin' moon will be the death of us.'

At the end of the year the young officer was in reflective mood.

30 December, 1917.

My dearest folks,

... A few weeks of this game makes a man think deeply on what is the meaning of life. If this ends all war, why every man should die very, very happy, but if it stops prematurely, and everyone starts preparing for the next, though we would fight just as well and hard—for it is for our country—yet in the back of our heads would still be the question, 'Why, oh why, should these millions of men have gone for nothing?' For it would seem the result were not worth the cost.

A provident soldier, Wood took out insurance of £10,000 to be divided between his parents and his sweetheart. Perhaps he had a premonition of death. 'If I am slated to go west, let it be in a big show with all the guns red-hot and the Huns piled upon the wire,' he wrote on 1 April, 1918. He had his big show at Château Thierry, 6–7 June, 1918, and won the Distinguished Service Cross for heroism. He was killed in action on 18 July near Soissons while in acting command of the Machine Gun Company of the 9th Infantry Regulars.

'They are still passing the buck'

The letters of Thomas H. Slussor are permeated with dissatisfaction against inefficiency in the American Army; he poured out his grievances to his wife, nearly always addressing her 'My dear little girl' and signing himself, 'Your lover, Harry.' Slussor became a captain of infantry, survived the war and died in the 1930s.

Base Hospital,
11 August, 1918.

Dearest, darlingest, forgive me for worrying you with all this trouble [as usual he had been critical of 'politics' in the Army and of inefficiency]. Do not fear, *I am coming back to you anyway*, but would like to feel, after the war, that I had been able to exercise as much power for the common good as many men of lesser ability or inclination might have exercised but did not.

I do not regret in any way coming into the Army in this Great Fight. It was the right thing to do. My only regret is that through a foolish prejudice I did not at once move every influence possible so that I might exercise the widest authority. Getting things done in the army is not a mysterious affair. It is only a matter of being blind in all directions of rank and personal advancement, possessing a single-minded determination to make things move and a hot intolerance for all inefficiency. . . . They are still passing the buck in my outfit as to why the men only got two cooked meals in 10 days, causing more damage by way of dysentery than from German bullets. . . . The food should have been brought to the men even if it left a train of manslaughter and courtmartial proceedings.

'Nothing too great to give'

Charles Hastings Upton, born in Boston, 4 September, 1893, served in the American 50th Aero Squadron, First Observation Group and was killed in an accident 28 August, 1918. In several letters to his family he confessed that war had brought him a realization of the existence of a 'Supreme Being'. The following letter was written in July 1918.

There is something more awe inspiring about an airplane crash than any other accident that may cause death. . . . I thought I had become hardened to death—I am not—my desire to fly is still with me. I do not fear my own death; there is too much beyond; but I fear to see my brothers go. And from all these accidents, sometimes fatal and sometimes not, a chap, even while seeing the injustice of it, gains a greater faith in what before may have seemed an intangible Supreme Being. It is paradoxical to have a greater faith in a Supreme Being who allows men to be killed, but it works that way.

Who can stand beside the open grave of a comrade, hear the volleys fired, and the sweet notes of 'Taps' [the American equivalent of *The Last Post*], see the airplanes swoop down to drop garlands over the spot, without feeling that there is something Greater? As the last note of 'Taps' sounds out over the spot, one has a vision, if you like, of a soul gone to a well-earned rest and to happiness. . . . And so through it all, we have our Grand Ideal, which tells us we have the glorious chance to grasp the opportunity of our lives, and if we come through, something to remember all our remaining days. For my part, I have never prepared to do anything comparable to what my service offers, I have never experienced anything of equal exaltation; in a word, service in a cause like ours becomes so absorbing, so impersonal, it grips one until there is *nothing too great to give, no sacrifice too great to make* for that which is now *sacred* to us. I hope I have given you something of the spirit of the boys over here, for we are all in the same situation, all in the same cause, all with the same Big Ideal. It's the greatest experience of our lives. I don't think we will lose the vision. . . . How could one lose his vision *at the front*, where if men are winged over the Biggest Top, they have gone with their Grand Ideal locked in their hearts.

'Our mothers think all of us fellows are roughnecks—see?'

Army chaplains were in a unique position to observe the effect of war on soldiers but surprisingly few of their letters are extant. Those of Gustav Stearns, Captain-Chaplain of the U.S. 127th Infantry Regiment in France, reveal much of the relationship between an American chaplain and his troops. He was writing to his congregation back home.

8 October, 1918.

The weather conditions were favorable the first and second Sunday I was in this camp, and the church services were conducted outdoors. The attendance was very satisfactory. The announcement of the services was made thru military channels, which means that notices were sent from the adjutant's office to

'There is just one little thing I fear'

William Cyrus Speakman, an educated and articulate American soldier, saw America's participation in the war with much more balance than many of his comrades. A major, Speakman was anxious that his countrymen should not claim too great a contribution to the war. As he survived the war he must have seen that his anxiety was justified.

14 October, 1918.

Not so very long ago a doughboy [slang term for the American soldier] with a sense of humor coined the expression, 'Heaven, Hell, or Hoboken by Christmas.' This morning the expression looks more like a fact than a joke. Within the past few days there appeared upon the front page of an American daily, a cartoon, the subject of which was, as it is of so many, 'The Kaiser'. The foundation was the globe, our earth; there were two figures, Uncle Sam and the Kaiser. Uncle Sam's hobnailed boot on his strong right foot had just been planted upon that portion of the Kaiser's anatomy he uses when sitting in State. Underneath were the words, 'Get off the earth'.

Now there is just one little thing I fear. I might almost call it our danger, and it's a precipice over which I pray we shall not stumble. Our danger is that we may loudly say, 'We did it.' We did do some of it, it is true. We figured in it, figured in it largely, but we didn't do it all; we just helped.

The French have never, for a moment, lost the spirit of the Marne, of Champagne and of Verdun. I don't think there ever was a moment when they did not think ultimate victory would be theirs. Even now, today, there is lots of fight in them. The English, to express it in the English way, can yet take a lot of beating. Belgium has thrown in a few parting shots just for luck, and poor little beaten and battered Serbia has moved up towards the King row; as for us, we also helped.

The picture of the aftermath is not a hard one to imagine. The long, straight, tree-lined roads, shell-holed everywhere; shell hole touching shell hole are everywhere strewed with wheels of carts and trucks, Boche hats and helmets, stacks of abandoned guns and caissons, ammunition by the ton, all left behind, so rapidly did the hob-nailed boot administer the propelling force; spectre walls are all that's left,—all that could be left.

A little farther back, the back areas of the Boches, the area where they had, as they thought, so strongly fortified themselves, sides of hills are full of dug-outs, many with fanciful fronts, many with not unattractive interior decorations. One I saw, with front of beams and cement, had a timbered effect,— I think the English call it. Inside, a gray-brown mattress webbing had been fashioned upon the pine walls to imitate burlap decorations. The whole was stripped in squares with pine strips, beautifully stained brown. There were arbors, summer houses if you will, built of rustic pine, bark still on. Around the bend of the hill, facing east, backs to the Allies, was a cemetery. An abrupt slope had been selected on the upper borders of the hills. They left the white birch trees, which are native in that sector; the graves in rows, terraced in the center and at the extreme back, they had built a monument of stone. On its upper portion, the Maltese Cross stood and, in bold relief, on the top of the monument, the Prussian Eagle, with out-stretched wings; directly in the center and on its widest part, the words: 'für Gott und Koenig und Vaterland'.

Every grave had its flat earth top, grassed sides, and every grave had a rose bush; many had stones, some not inartistically carved; one, an open Bible carved out of wood. Periwinkle was running among the ivy, and in the center of it all, a big bed of the handsomest Kaiserin Augusta Victoria roses I ever saw.

I stood there a long time. I could not help admiring the flowers; they were perfect specimens, and the whole cemetery was, to say the least, artistically made. A few hundred yards away, shells were breaking below, and to the right, what was at one time a town, but now only spectre walls. A little French cemetery, a few hundred yards away, with rusting gate, paths and graves overgrown with weeds,—quite a difference. Not a flower, not a vine, not a rose! Of course there were no French behind that line; all was Boches and their ruin. But the ruins are not the ruins of yesterday, the vines and wreaths told the tale of four years ago.

During one of my runs over into ex-Boche-land, I saw a drawer from a filing system, not very large. It was lying on the ground, wires cut. I wish I had gathered it in. It was most ingeniously arranged to go off when the drawer was pulled out. I do not know the case from which the drawer was taken. I gathered in a lot of letters from the home folks, one a love letter and a German newspaper of August 8th. I wish I could send them to you. You would have fun with them. I am going to send you one of the tin hats. Men are sending them home. Some have reached their destination; others have not. Perhaps thousands are sent home and that's why all do not reach their destination. I am sorry our postal system is so, for there is so much I want to send. I simply cannot carry them about with me. The motto in the A.E.F. [American Expeditionary Force] is, 'Travel light'. My bedding roll and a barracks bag are the sum total of my luggage.

Speakman's letter effectively scotches the oft-expressed assertion that the Germans had no regard for their battle dead and either left them to rot or interred them in anonymous mass graves.

'*Oh boy, it was some sport!*'

A letter written by Sergeant Victor Vigorito is typical of the approach of men in the ranks—ebullient, aggressive and rather vainglorious. The sergeant had no doubt that the Americans had come to France to show their allies how to fight. Born in Brooklyn, Vigorito became well known as a boxer under the name of Johnny Victor. As a member of the 1st Battalion, 325th Infantry Regiment, he fought at Toul, St Mihiel, Norroy, St Juvin and Argonne Forest. Wounded on 15 October, 1918, he was cited for 'great bravery and devotion'. He wrote to friends to answer their queries about his war experiences.

War now came to us with a vengeance. We had a long stretch of front to hold by ourselves. The enemy was active and aggressive, and we were there to punish him. Patrol work gave us a great opportunity.

The southern boys certainly showed up like stars in this work, and by sending city men with them, the whole gang soon learned how to creep out in the dark and stalk a German patrol or listening post. It got so finally, that our men would slip out on their own hook, stalk a German, kill him with a trench knife, and bring his helmet or cap for a trophy. Oh, boy! It was some sport.

Trench raids were our meat, too. You know how they go. The artillery sneak up a bunch of guns and get them all registered on a few hundred yards of German trench. The men who are to make the raid are given plenty of opportunity to look over the ground so they'll know it in the dark. Zero hour comes along.

Whoop! A box barrage comes down on Mr. Hun, cuts him off from retreat, and prevents reinforcements from getting up.

The raiding party nurses its bombs and grenades in eager hands, makes sure the knives are loose and ready to hand, and then springs over the top; stumbles along toward the German line, rips its clothing to pieces on the wire, cut by the shelling, loses a few men in the crossing,—to whet its appetite for the slaughter,—takes a deep breath, and springs into the enemy's first line, stinking of fresh spilled blood, greasy with the flesh spewed all over by the shell.

A German officer comes running along. An automatic sticks out a tongue of pinkish yellow fire and acrid gas. The Hun crumples.

Some one is crying: 'Kamerad! Kamerad!' The fellow does not show himself, and we are just naturally suspicious. They give him a grenade and he stops his bleating. Meanwhile parties of Huns have been cornered in the dugouts. The officers look the dugouts over and figure out how many men will be in them and then:

'Four.'

'Six.' Or some such number is spoken quietly. A sergeant steps forward and counts out the required number of pills [high-explosive grenades]. The men fall back the least bit, and the grenades are tossed into the dugouts.

The party runs right over one fellow who is hiding.

An officer speaks up quickly. 'Don't give it to him! Take him back, a couple of you. We'll see what he knows.'

A quick search follows for papers or anything that will give us valuable information.

Then back we go.

Going back it is lively, for the Huns have opened up on the ground we have to cross, and in the trenches to the right and left of the raided sector, the men are alert and throwing up flares.

We duck, dodge, creep, crawl, and finally get back.

A few of the boys have got it on the way back, but we have brought them all along.

The Big Fellow up at G.H.Q. looks over the report and a smile lights up his grim old face. 'Pretty good stuff in the Eighty-second! Send them along with the First and Second! They can travel in fast company.'

On the 9th of August, we are on the move, just in time to miss a big gas attack.

We go to Pont-a-Musson and relieve,—just think of it—the Eighty-second relieves the Second Division! [An élite division.] We spit on our hands and square our shoulders then, I'll tell the country.

The Second had put the fear of the Americans into the hearts of the Hun, and it was comparatively quiet.

Then on the 12th, old John Joseph Pershing [General Pershing, American Commander-in-Chief] just says to the Eighty-second: 'Go and get 'em. That's what you came for!'

I don't mean to say, he said that to us in person, but he said it all right in his orders,—only in military language, you know, all dressed up for the histories.

They told us, our officers did, before we went in, that this was the first time the American had gone it all alone. They told us we came over to win the war, and this was our chance. They told us, not to let the Huns get away from us, if we had to run our damned legs off.

In we went and did what we were told to do; and then some. For five days and nights we never stopped. Of course, the same men were not fighting all the time, but the Division was, and the relief any bunch got was only a few hours, then they would be at it again.

I'd like to describe that for you, but I can't seem to do it, yet, it is so confused, as though you had been in a glorified riot for five days and nights. You couldn't describe such a thing.

We took Norroy, and I'd say that was some fight. German aeroplanes flying around overhead firing at us with machine guns; the Huns in the town blazing away.

Well, we took the town. But we lost a bunch of guys there. Now and then, we took a few prisoners, but we had no time for any la-de-da business with the Huns. Mostly, they got the bayonet or grenade. We strewed the ground with them plenty—I'd say we did.

Having done so well at St Mihiel, G.H.Q. decided to give us a rest, so they sent us to the Argonne Forest. The rest consisted of relieving the Twenty-eighth Division, establishing a new position by taking a crossing of the Aisne near Appremont, and then pushing along with our battle line astride of the Aisne.

There was some great killing pulled off there, both by the Germans and ourselves. We sent several German divisions to the rear with the very life whaled out of them, while the numbers of our men were so reduced that two regiments must be united to make even one small one.

Each day our orders were the same. 'Push steadily on, regardless of the cost. Hold what you take, and keep up with the enemy.'

The orders were obeyed, though our men fell by hundreds. The Division was being annihilated, but those of us who were left never thought of quitting; we were killing too many Huns each day to think much about what was happening to us.

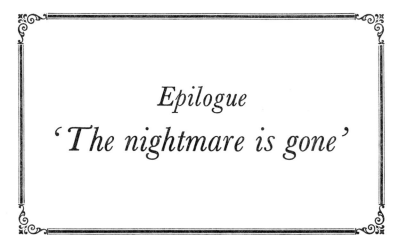

Epilogue
'The nightmare is gone'

Canadian Lieutenant A. G. A. Vidler, M.C., expressed the sentiments of many soldiers in a letter written home on 13 November, 1918—two days after the Armistice. Having spent four years at the war Vidler has a particular right to the last word.

Just going on leave! Only a few lines to let you know I am O.K. and was in the line by Mons-Maubeuge when the Armistice was signed and hostilities ceased . . . I was in the last big show on 4th November, when this regiment took Wagnieres-le-Grand, with 300 prisoners, 20 machine-guns and 5 trench mortars.

After that the Hun was done for, and we marched night and day to the Mons-Charleroi road, via Malplaquet and then he threw up the sponge. Great days! and the best two months' war I have ever known, chasing him from town to town. I have a good sword, automatic revolver and field glasses as trophies from the last battle at Villers Pol on 4th November, where his machine-gunners put up a stiff fight. We were helped by a ground mist and literally jumped on trenches full of Huns, who either surrendered or ran like hares. Anyhow it's all finished, thank God! The nightmare of four and a half years is gone.

Acknowledgments

Despite exhaustive attempts, I have not been able to trace the copyright owners of many letters produced in this book. In the majority of cases copyright has expired, but as a courtesy I tried to locate the writer, his heirs or—in some cases—earlier publishers. The publishers and I would be grateful for information about the whereabouts of the holders of any copyright letter not acknowledged here, in particular for the address of the heirs of Colonel Rowland Feilding.

My grateful thanks are due to various people in connection with letters written by the following soldiers:

Greenwell, Graham: Mr Greenwell himself and Allen Lane The Penguin Press, who republished his book, *An Infant In Arms*, in 1972.

Heath, Arthur George: Mr Basil Blackwell wrote (11 April, 1972): 'I am sorry I cannot put you in touch with the literary executor or assign of Arthur Heath. He had a sister I remember half a century ago. I am sure she would approve your quoting her brother's letters; he was a noble creature. May I vicariously give you full permission.'

Henderson, Keith: Writing to me in April 1972 to give permission to quote from his *Letters to Helen* (1917) this indomitable gentleman said, 'I wrote to my darling sweet one, whom I have recently lost, every day. . . .'

The Love of an Unknown Soldier (anon.) to John Lane Ltd (The Bodley Head).

Jeffares, R. J.: Williams, J. S.; Thompson, D. S.

Stearns, Gustav: Augsburg Publishing House, Minneapolis.

Upton, Charles Hastings: Houghton Mifflin Co., New York.

Vidler, A. G. A.: The Canadian Imperial Bank of Commerce, Toronto. In 1920 the bank published two large volumes of letters written by staff members who had joined the forces.

Woodward, Houston: Yale Publishing Association, New Haven, Connecticut.

The letters of Ivar Campbell, Llewellyn Jones, T. M. Kettle, J. L. Rapoport, D. O. Barnett, W. H. Ratcliffe and H. S. Lawson first appeared in *War Letters of Fallen Englishmen*, 1930. The publishers, Victor Gollancz Ltd, referred me to A. M. Heath & Co., London, the literary agents, but I was unable to obtain a reply to my queries.

Many letters written by soldiers who died during the war were privately printed in book form in small numbers. I have written to the printers, where shown, but none could give me an address of the owners. This applies particularly to the letters of:

Caspar Burton (Cambridge, Massachusetts, 1921); William Cyrus Speakman (Wilmington, Delaware, 1937); Thomas H. Slussor (Chicago, 1937); Philip Russell Keightley (Belfast, probably 1920); Henry Bentinck (London, 1919); Walter Bertram Wood and Edwin Leonard Wood (Grimsby, probably 1920); Lambert Wood (Portland, Oregon, 1936).

Index

Aero Squadron, American 50th, 117
Agar-Robartes, Captain the Hon. Thomas, 91
Agny, 61
Aisne, river, 57, 107, 126
Aldag, Karl, 27–9
Aldershot, 48
Alexandria, 44
Allen, Lieutenant John Hugh, 38–9
American Ambulance, 110
— Army, views on, 110–15, 116, 118, 121, 123
— Civil War, 111
— Expeditionary Force, 123
Ancre, river, 61, 107
Anderson, Major Francis Sainthill, 76–9
anonymous French soldier, 7, 11, 21–6
— writer of love letters, 102–5
Anzacs (Australian and New Zealand Army Corps), 39, 55
Appremont, 126
'Archies' (anti-aircraft shells), 85
Argonne Forest, 123, 126

Argyll and Sutherland Highlanders, 10, 11
Armistice (1918), 127
Army Service Corps, 68
Arras, 61, 75
Art and Opportunity, 10
Auchel, 99
Australian Light Horse Regiment, 14th, 39, 41
— — — —, 5th, 41, 42
Avord, 111
awards for bravery, unfair distribution of, 98–101

Bairnsfather, Captain Bruce, 77, 115–16
Bapaume, 72
Barnett, Lieutenant Denis Oliver, 33–4, 129
Bassée, La, 10, 12, 90
Belloy-en-Santerre, 17
Benson, H., 39
Bentinck, Major Henry, 34–7, 129
Bethune, 90
Blackwell, Basil, 128
Bonneville, 65
Bruhn, Private Eduard, 6, 11

Bryson, Captain, 62
Bunyan, John, 15
Burton Jr, First-Lieutenant Caspar Henry, 113–14, 129

Callaway, Robert Furley, 67
Cambrin, 90
Campbell, Captain Ivar, 9, 11, 37, 129
Canadian Expeditionary Force, 107
Caudron bi-plane, 112
Champagne, 18, 25, 60, 121
Chapin, Lance-Corporal Harold, 6, 10, 30–3
Charleroi, 127
Château Thierry, 116
Churchill, Sir Winston, 48
Civil Service Rifles, 1st, 90
Clamency, 15
Cluses, 65
Clutton-Brock, A. C., 21
'Coal boxes' (heavy shells), 50, 58–9
Coldstream Guards, 35, 90
Combres, Heights of, 26
Connaught Rangers, 90
Corot, 65
Corps Expéditionnaire d'Orient, 43
Cuthbert, Captain Harold, 92–3

Daily Telegraph, 17
Dardanelles, 45
Desborough, Lady, 11
Desborough, Lord, 11
Döberitz, 26
Douve, river, 53
Doyle, Sir Arthur Conan, 71
Dumb and the Blind, The, 10
dysentery among American troops, 117

Egerton, Major A. G. E., 93
Egypt, 35

Eleonte, 44
Engall, Second-Lieutenant John Sherwin, 6, 11
Eparges, Les, 26
Ervillers, 95, 96

Feilding, Lieutenant-Colonel Rowland, 90–101
Festubert, 66
Flanders, 33, 81, 86
Foch, Field Marshal Ferdinand, 108
fraternization between British and German troops, 28–9, 35, 94–5
French, General Sir John, 35
French Flying Corps, 111, 112
— Foreign Legion, 17
Fromelles, 28

Gaba Tepe, 40
Gallipoli, 38, 39, 43, 55
Garnett, Lieutenant Kenneth Gordon, 7, 11
Garvey, Captain Ivan, 93
gas, poison, 34, 80
Gibson, Alan K., Transport Officer, 52
Gillespie, Second-Lieutenant A. D., 3–4, 10, 12–15, 48
Goodyear, Lieutenant Hedley John, 107–8
Gordon Highlanders, 29
Greenwell, Captain Graham, 51–7, 65, 128
Grenadier Guards, 29, 35
Grenfell, Gerald, 11
Grenfell, Captain the Hon. Julian Henry Francis, 7, 11
Grouchy, Major Joseph de, 43
Guinchy, 35

Haas, Johannes, 60–1
Hamilton, General Sir Ian, 69
Hampshire Regiment, 85

'Happy Warrior', 15
Havre, Le, 106
Heath, Lieutenant Arthur George, 45–9, 128
Hébuterne, 54
Hellwich, hero, 69–70
Henderson, Helen, 10
Henderson, Captain Keith, 5, 10, 128
Hersin, 75
Hewett, Second-Lieutenant Stephen, 3n., 62–5
Hindenburg Line, 55
Hobson, Second-Lieutenant Vincent, 64
Hogue, Major Oliver ('Trooper Bluegum'), 39–42
Holly Ridge, 40
hospital conditions for the army, 73–6

Infant In Arms, An, 128
Infantry Regiment, U.S. 127th, 118
— —, U.S. 325th, 123
— Regulars, 9th, 116
Intelligence Corps, 10
Into Battle, 11
Ireland, troubles in, 70–1
Isle-Adam, Villiers de L', 22
Italian front, 57, 77–9
It's the Poor that 'Elps the Poor, 10

'Jack Johnsons' (heavy shells), 58–9
Jeffares, Corporal R. J., 49–50, 129
Jones, Captain John Llewellyn Thomas, 81–2, 129

Keightley, Captain Philip Russell, 86–8, 129
Kemmel, 58
Kettle, Captain Thomas Michael, 70, 71, 129

King's Regiment, 4th, 113

Lancashire Fusiliers, 108
Lane, John, 102
Lawson, Lieutenant Harry Sackville, 82–4, 129
Legien, 61
Leinster Regiment, 33
Leintrey, 59
Lempire, 97
Letters to Helen, 128
Lewis machine-gun, 67, 97, 98
Liebknecht, Karl, 61
Litzmann, General Karl, 73
London Regiment, 3rd, 81
— —, 15th, 65
— —, 16th, 6, 11
Loos, 10, 15
Love Letters of an Anzac, 39
Love of an Unknown Soldier, The, 129
Luard, Sister K. E., 73
Lucas, Major Travers, 80
Lusitania, 19

Magneux, 18
Malplaquet, 127
Marne, river, 121
Marseilles, 43
Maubeuge, 127
Mesopotamia, 11
Messines Ridge, 58
Mondidier, 111
Mons, 13, 127
Moroccan Division, 2nd, 19
Müller, Heinrich, 71–2, 73
Müller, Hugo, 61–2
Murray, Professor Sir Gilbert, 45, 48
Murray, Lady Mary, 48

New South Wales Lancers, 40
Nijni Novgorod, 48
Nivelle Offensive, 57
Norroy, 123, 125

Northcliffe, Lord (Alfred Harmsworth), 48
Nottingham, Sergeant Ernest Boughton, 65-6

'Old Bill' (cartoon character), 77, 116
'One crowded hour', 14
Officers' Training Corps (Glasgow), 14
— — — (Harvard), 114
Ovillers, 54
Oxfordshire and Buckinghamshire Light Infantry, 51
Paris, 72
Pas de Calais, 99
Pereira, General George Edward, 94
Pershing, General John Joseph, 125
Pilgrim's Progress, 15
'Pirates of Penzance, The', 46
Ploegsteert Wood, 51
Polish-Galician salient, 13
Ponsonby, Major-General Sir John, 90
Pont-à-Musson, 125
Pretoria, Bishop of, 48
Public Schools Officers' Camp, 51

Rapoport, Second-Lieutenant John Lindsay, 105-7, 129
Ratcliffe, Second-Lieutenant William Henry, 68-9, 129
Red Cross, American, 102, 114
Redmond, Major William Hoey Kearney, 70-1
Regiment, German 165th, 72-3
Reims, 17, 25
Rifle Brigade, 106
Roche, La, 65
Roy, Walter, 26-7
Royal Army Medical Corps, 6, 10

— Dragoons, 11
— Dublin Fusiliers, 70
— Engineers, 80
— Field Artillery, 11, 76, 82
— Flying Corps, 84, 85
— Fusiliers, 113
— Garrison Artillery, 86
— Horse Artillery ('Eagle Troop'), 76
— Irish Constabulary, 100
— — Regiment, 71
— Military Academy, 89
— Scots Fusiliers, 1st, 85
— West Kent Regiment, 45
Russian front, 11, 13, 72

St Ives, Douve Valley, 53
St Juvin, 123
St Menehould, 112
St Mihiel, 26, 123, 126
Sallanches, 65
Samain, Albert, 22
Savoie, 43
Scheidemann, Philipp, 61
Schwinjuchy, 72
Scots Guards, 29, 92
Scott, Sir Walter, 14
Secretan, Hubert, 62-4
Seeger, Alan, 17-20
Serbia, 121
Sherman, General William T., 110, 111
Sherwood Foresters, 11, 67
Simpson, Lieutenant Henry Lamont, 108-9
Slussor, Captain Thomas H., 116-17, 129
Sohnrey, Friedrich (Fidus), 15-16
Somme, river, 6, 54, 62, 67, 68, 69, 71, 77, 86, 107
South African War, 40
— Staffordshire Regiment, 68
Spanbrok-Molen, 58

Speakman, Major William
    Cyrus, 121–3, 129
Stearns, Captain/Chaplain
    Gustav, 118–20, 129
Stegemann, Lieutenant Hans,
    72–3
Sudan, the, 35

Taube plane, 50
Templer, Captain Claude, 89
Thompson, Captain D. S., 80–1
Times, The, 48
Toul, 123
Toulon, 43
Turks, 40, 41, 42

Upton, Charles Hastings, 117–
    118, 129
Urquhart, F. F., 64

Vaeth, Alfred, 59–60, 65
Verdun, 19, 22, 25, 60, 121
Vidler, Lieutenant A. G. A.,
    127, 129
Vigorito, Sergeant Victor, 123–6
Villers Pol, 127
Vimy Ridge, 74, 75, 80
Vosges, German, 22

Wagnières-le-Grand, 127
War Letters of Fallen Englishmen,
    129

Warlencourt, 61
Warsaw, 93
Wellington, 1st Duke of (Arthur
    Wellesley), 39
Wilhelm II, Kaiser, 121
Williams, Charles, 65
Williams, Lieutenant J. S., 58–9,
    129
Wilson, Captain Theodore
    Percival Cameron, 8, 11
Woëvre, 26
Wood, Dorothy, 85
Wood, Second-Lieutenant Edwin
    Leonard, 85, 86, 129
Wood, Lieutenant Lambert,
    114–16, 129
Wood, Lieutenant Walter
    Bertram, 85–6, 129
Woodward, Houston, 110–13
Worcestershire Regiment, 38
Wordsworth, William, 15, 109
Workers' Educational Associa-
    tion, 45
World War, Second, 4, 57

Ypres, 31, 34, 86

Zeppelins, 5
Zulu War, 40